DAYBOOK

OF CRITICAL READING AND WRITING

daybook, *n.* a book in which the events of the day are recorded; *specif.* a journal or diary

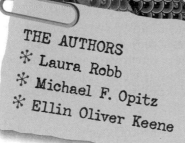

THE AUTHORS
* Laura Robb
* Michael F. Opitz
* Ellin Oliver Keene

Great Source Education Group
A division of Houghton Mifflin Company
Wilmington, Massachusetts

THE AUTHORS

✳ **Laura Robb** has more than forty years of classroom experience in grades 4 through 8. Robb also coaches teachers in grades K to 12 in school districts in her home state of Virginia, New York, and Michigan and speaks at conferences throughout the country. Author of more than fifteen books for teachers, Robb's latest title is *Teaching Reading: A Complete Resource for Grades Four and Up* (Scholastic, 2006). For Great Source, Robb has developed, with other authors, *Reading Advantage, Writing Advantage, and Reader's Handbook* for grades 3 to 8.

✳ **Michael F. Opitz** is Professor of Reading at the University of Northern Colorado, where he teaches graduate and undergraduate literacy courses. He is the author or coauthor of several books including *Diagnosis and Improvement in Reading Instruction,* 5th ed. (Allyn & Bacon, 2007), *Books and Beyond* (Heinemann, 2006), *Listen, Hear!* (Heinemann, 2005), and *Goodbye Round Robin* (Heinemann, 1998) as well as the reading programs *Afterschool Achievers: Reading Club* (Great Source, 2004) and *Literacy By Design* (Harcourt, 2007).

✳ **Ellin Oliver Keene** has been a classroom teacher, staff developer, and adjunct professor of reading and writing. For sixteen years, she directed staff development initiatives at the Denver-based Public Education & Business Coalition. She served as Deputy Director and Director of Literacy and Staff Development for the Cornerstone Project at the University of Pennsylvania for four years. Ellin is co-author of *Mosaic of Thought: Teaching Comprehension in a Readers' Workshop* (Heinemann, 1997), the second edition of which will be released in 2007. She is also the author of *To Understand* (Heinemann, 2007) and *Assessing Comprehension Thinking Strategies* (Shell Educational Books, 2006).

REVIEWERS

Cheryl N. Chance
Houston, TX

Caroline Goodnight
Elk Grove, CA

Pickett Pat Lema, Ed.D.
St. Louis County, MO

Anne Patin
Lafayette, LA

EDITORIAL: Ruth Rothstein and Sue Paro
DESIGN AND PRODUCTION: AARTPACK, Inc.

Printed in the United States of America

International Standard Book Number 13: 978-0-669-54978-2

International Standard Book Number 10: 0-669-54978-9

2 3 4 5 6 7 8 9 10   0914   12 11 10

Contents

Focus / Skill		Selection / Author	

Focus / Skill	Selection / Author	

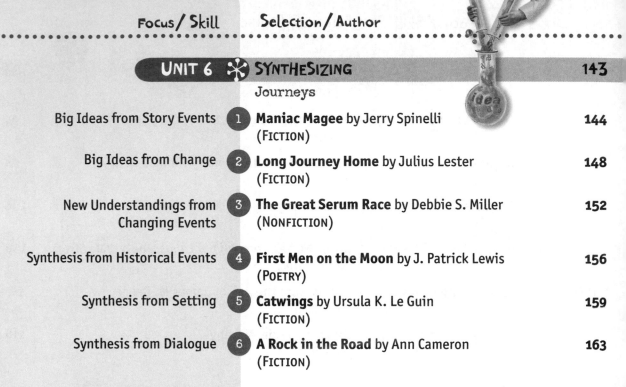

Important!

Date and name

Becoming an Active Reader

The best way to become a great athlete is to be as active as you can—even when you're sitting still. When you're not playing your sport, watch others who are, and think about their decisions and strategies.

Reading is a lot like playing a sport. The more you read actively, the better you'll get. As an active reader, you interact with the text by thinking, writing, and talking about it.

The strategy lessons in this Daybook will build your reading power. In each unit, you'll interact with the text by making connections, asking questions, determining importance, visualizing, making inferences, and synthesizing. By actively using these strategies, you'll understand, remember, and enjoy what you read.

When you read, look for ideas and details that remind you of things you already know. This is called making connections. **Making connections** with a text will help you better understand and remember what you read. Make connections by asking questions such as these:

- What does this remind me of?
- Where have I seen or heard this before?

Practice making connections with the folktale *How Spider Got a Thin Waist*. Mark the text by underlining phrases or sentences that remind you of things you already know. Explain your connections in the **Response Notes**.

Response Notes

This reminds me of a story about how the leopard got his spots.

How Spider Got a Thin Waist

retold by Joyce Cooper Arkhurst

Many dry seasons ago, before the oldest man in our village can remember, before the rain and the dry and the rain and the dry that any one of us can talk about to his children, Spider was a very big person. He did not look as he looks today, with his fat head and his fat body and his thin waist in between. Of course, he had two eyes and eight legs and he lived in a web. But none of him was thin. He was big and round, and his waistline was very fat indeed. Today, he is very different, as all of you know, and this is how it came to pass.

One day Spider was walking through the forest. It was early morning and he noticed an unusually pleasant smell. He wrinkled his nose and sniffed the wind. It was food! Goodness! He had almost forgotten.

Ask questions before, during, and after reading. **Asking questions** keeps you interested in the reading because you search for the answers. Through questioning, your thinking becomes clearer.

As you read, ask questions such as these:

- What will happen next?

- Why did that character do that?

- Why did the author include (or not include) those details?

As you continue reading the folktale, underline or circle parts of the text that raise questions or cause you to question the author. Write your questions in the **Response Notes**.

How Spider Got a Thin Waist *continued*

Today was the festival of the harvest. Every village in the big forest was preparing a feast. The women were cooking yams and cassava, and chicken with peanut-flavored sauce. There would be fish and peppers and rice boiling in the great pots over the fires.

Spider's heart jumped for joy. His mouth watered. His eyes sparkled and he smiled brightly. Already he could taste the food on his tongue.

Now, of course, Spider had not done any of the work to deserve such a feast, and no one had invited him to come and eat. Spider had not planted yam or potato. He had not planted rice, nor gone to sea in a long boat to catch fish. For Spider did not like to work at all. All day he played in the sun or slept, and since it is not the custom to refuse food to anyone who comes to one's door, he could eat very well by simply visiting all his friends. In fact, he ate more than they did.

Response Notes

What is cassava?

I think spider is going to get himself into trouble.

As you read, you pause at times to **determine which details and ideas are important.** You use your background knowledge, opinions, and purpose for reading to help you make your choices. Your choices may be different from someone else's.

As you read the next part of the folktale, notice the details the author includes about Spider. Underline the most important sentences, phrases, and words. Explain your choices in the **Response Notes.**

Response Notes

Spider thought of a solution to his problem.

How Spider Got a Thin Waist *continued*

Now Spider was right in the middle of the forest. Not far away there were two villages. Spider stood just in the middle, and the two were exactly the same distance away. Today each village would have a great feast.

"How lucky for me!" thought Spider.

But then he was puzzled. Since there were two dinners, he did not know which one he wanted to go to. That is, he did not know which would have the most to eat. So Spider sat under a breadfruit tree and thought and thought and thought. <u>At last he had an idea! He could go to them both!</u> Of course. Spider was so pleased with his good idea that he did a little dance right there and then.

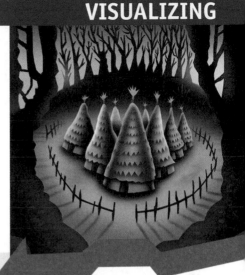

hen you read, certain words and phrases create **sensory images** in your mind. A sensory image can make you feel as though you see, hear, feel, taste, or smell something. These images help you **visualize** and understand what you're reading.

As you read the next part of the folktale, underline words and phrases that spark your emotions and create sensory images. In the **Response Notes**, write about or draw the images you see and feel while reading.

How Spider Got a Thin Waist *continued*

But how could he know when the food was ready? He sat under the breadfruit tree again and thought and thought and thought. And then he had another idea. <u>He did another little dance just because he was so brilliant.</u> And then he did two things.

First, he called his eldest son, Kuma. He took a long rope and tied one end around his waist. The other end he gave to his son.

"Take this rope to the village on the East," he said to Kuma. "When the food is ready, give the rope a hard pull, and I will know it is time for me to come and eat."

And so Kuma went to the East village and took the end of the rope with him.

Then Spider called his youngest son, Kwaku. He took another long rope and tied it around his waist, just below the first one.

"Kwaku, take this rope to the village on the West," he said, "and when the food is all cooked, pull very hard on it. Then I will come and have my fill."

Response Notes

I imagine Spider
dancing with a
big smile.

Authors don't include every possible detail when they write. They purposely leave out bits of information that they expect you to **infer**, or figure out. In a text, look for clues that reveal hidden details the author doesn't state. When you combine these clues with your own thoughts to create new information, you are **making an inference**. An inference can be a conclusion, an interpretation, or a prediction. Making inferences will deepen your understanding of a text.

As you read the next section of the folktale, infer what you think will happen next. Underline sentences and phrases that spark your inferences. Write your inferences in the **Response Notes**.

Spider is going to be squeezed!

How Spider Got a Thin Waist *continued*

So Kwaku went to the West village, carrying the end of the rope with him.

My friends, can you image what happened? I don't think so, so I will tell you. The people in the East village and the people in the West village had their dinners at *exactly the same time.* So, of course, Kuma and Kwaku pulled on both of the ropes at the same time. <u>Kuma pulled to the East and Kwaku pulled to the West. The ropes got tighter and tighter.</u> Poor, greedy Spider was caught in the middle. He could go neither east nor west, nor left nor right.

s you read and reread a text, your thoughts and ideas change. You learn new information that affects how you think or feel about a piece. As your thoughts and ideas change, you **synthesize**, or create, new understandings. Often these new understandings are big ideas or themes the author is trying to get across.

When you finish the folktale, reread the Response Notes for the entire selection. Think about the twists and turns your mind took along the way. Then review all your thoughts and feelings about the piece to synthesize some big ideas or themes. Write your big ideas or themes in the **Response Notes**. Then share and discuss them with a partner.

How Spider Got a Thin Waist *continued*

Kuma and Kwaku could not understand why their father did not come, and they pulled harder all the time. And something was happening to Spider. The ropes squeezed tighter and tighter and his waist got thinner and thinner. Kuma and Kwaku waited until all the food was eaten. Then they came to look for their father. When they found him, he looked very different. His waistline was thinner than a needle! Spider never grew fat again. He stayed the same until today. He has a big head and a big body, and a tiny little waist in between. ❖

Think ahead before you make a decision!

Making Connections

You and a friend walk by a pet shop. You see a German shepherd puppy in the window. You say to your friend, "Maybe that dog will grow up to be a search-and-rescue dog. I saw a real search-and-rescue dog once, and it was a German shepherd."

You just used your own experience to **make a connection.** You compared something you saw with something you already knew.

When you read, you can make connections, too. In this unit, you will practice making connections with characters' thoughts, words, and actions. All the people and the characters you'll read about will be **following their dreams.**

CONNECTING WITH A POEM

When you make connections with a poem, the ideas in the poem will make more sense. To make connections as you read, ask yourself questions like these:

- What does this remind me of?
- Have I ever felt this way?
- How might this thought or idea inspire me?

The poem in this lesson is about holding on to your dreams. In the **Response Notes**, you will see how one reader made connections with the poem. Use your own thoughts or personal experiences to make connections with the poem.

Dreams by Langston Hughes

Hold fast to dreams
For if dreams die
Life is a broken-winged bird
That cannot fly.

Hold fast to dreams
For when dreams go
Life is a barren field
Frozen with snow. ❖

Response Notes

How do dreams die?

I had a dream about winning a race. I hope it comes true.

✳ What does this poem make you think about?

....

....

....

....

✳ Think about your own dreams. What dream do you
hope will come true by the end of fourth grade?
How will you accomplish it?

....

....

....

....

....

....

....

....

✻ Write a diary entry about a dream you'd like to accomplish when you grow up. How will you achieve your dream?

When you make personal connections with a poem, the poem will become more meaningful to you.

When you read a story, you might notice something familiar. Maybe something in the story happened to you. Maybe you wish you could speak with one of the characters. Thoughts like these are **personal connections**. Making personal connections with a story helps you better understand, enjoy, and remember what you read.

As you read the fiction story *Uncle Jed's Barbershop*, make personal connections with the text. Underline ideas in the story that connect with your own life. Write about the connections in the **Response Notes**.

from Uncle Jed's Barbershop
by Margaree King Mitchell

When I was five years old, I got sick. This particular morning, I didn't come into the kitchen while Mama was fixing breakfast. Mama and Daddy couldn't wake me up. My nightgown and the bedclothes were all wet where I had sweated.

Mama wrapped me in a blanket while Daddy went outside and hitched the horse to the wagon. We had to travel about twenty miles into town to the hospital. It was midday when we got there. We had to go to the colored waiting room. In those days, they kept blacks and whites separate. There were separate public rest rooms, separate water fountains, separate schools. It was called segregation. So in the hospital, we had to go to the colored waiting room.

Even though I was unconscious, the doctors wouldn't look at me until they had finished with all the white patients. When the doctors did examine me, they told my daddy that I needed an operation and that it would cost three hundred dollars.

Response Notes

Three hundred dollars was a lot of money in those days. My daddy didn't have that kind of money. And the doctors wouldn't do the operation until they had the money.

My mama bundled me back up in the blanket and they took me home. Mama held me in her arms all night. She kept me alive until Daddy found Uncle Jed. He found him early the next morning in the next county on his way to cut somebody's hair. Daddy told him about me.

Uncle Jed leaned on his bent cane and stared straight ahead. He told Daddy that the money didn't matter. He couldn't let anything happen to his Sarah Jean. ❖

What was the strongest personal connection you made with this selection? Explain.

COLORED

WAITING ROOM

✳ Tell about a time you or someone you know was treated differently than others. How did you feel? How did you resolve the problem?

....

....

....

....

....

....

....

....

....

....

....

Making personal connections with a story will help you understand, enjoy, and remember it.

You learn a lot about a character from his or her thoughts, words, and actions. By making connections with a character, you gain a greater understanding of the character's feelings and experiences.

In the first part of *Uncle Jed's Barbershop*, you learned that Sarah Jean needed an expensive operation. Her Uncle Jed paid for it.

As you read the rest of the story, underline sentences and phrases that give you clues about Uncle Jed's personality. In the **Response Notes**, write what the clues tell you about Uncle Jed and any connections you make with him.

Response Notes

from Uncle Jed's Barbershop
by Margaree King Mitchell

Well, I had the operation. For a long time after that, Uncle Jed came by the house every day to see how I was doing. I know that three hundred dollars delayed him from opening the barbershop.

Uncle Jed came awfully close to opening his shop a few years after my operation. He had saved enough money to buy the land and build the building. But he still needed money for the equipment.

Anyway, Uncle Jed had come by the house. We had just finished supper when there was a knock on the door. It was Mr. Ernest Walters, a friend of Uncle Jed's. He had come by to tell Uncle Jed about the bank failing. That was where Mr. Walters and Uncle Jed had their money. Uncle Jed had over three thousand dollars in the bank, and it was gone.

Uncle Jed just stood there a long time before he said anything. Then he told Mr. Walters that even though he was disappointed, he would just have to start all over again.

Talk about some hard times. That was the beginning of the Great Depression. Nobody had much money.

But Uncle Jed kept going around to his customers cutting their hair, even though they couldn't pay him. His customers shared with him whatever they had—a hot meal, fresh eggs, vegetables from the garden. And when they were able to pay again, they did.

And Uncle Jed started saving all over again.

Ol' Uncle Jed finally got his barbershop. He opened it on his seventy-ninth birthday. It had everything, just like he said it would—big comfortable chairs, four cutting stations. You name it! The floors were so clean, they sparkled.

On opening day, people came from all over the county. They were Ol' Uncle Jed's customers. He had walked to see them for so many years. That day they all came to him. ❖

✳ **In what ways do you connect with Uncle Jed? Explain.**

✳ Write two diary entries that Uncle Jed might have written about his dream of opening a barbershop. The first entry (below) should take place before the bank failed. The second entry (on page 25) should take place after the bank failed.

Before the bank failed,

After the bank failed,

✳ Look back at the two selections you have read in this unit. Which selection did you connect the most with? How did your connections help you better understand the selection?

I connected the most with . . .

My connections helped me by . . .

Making connections with a story character will help you understand his or her feelings and experiences.

Making connections with a real person can help you better understand the events and experiences in his or her life.

Sammy Lee was the first Asian American to win an Olympic gold medal, at the 1948 Games in London. This selection from Sammy Lee's **biography** takes you to the actual moment that Sammy fulfills his lifelong dream.

As you read, think about and underline Sammy's character traits, or words that describe his personality. In the **Response Notes**, write the names of the traits he has.

from Sixteen Years in Sixteen Seconds by Paula Yoo

Response Notes

Sammy stood on the diving board. He was sure everyone could hear his heart beating. Then he focused himself, jumped high, and made one of his best dives ever. It won him the bronze medal.

Sammy was happy but not satisfied. He wanted to win a gold medal. He knew his strength lay in the upcoming 10-meter platform event. Here was his chance to show he was the greatest diver in the world.

Right before the event, Sammy heard a rumor that there might be some prejudice against him because he wasn't white. This only added to his determination to win.

Sammy remained calm. "I'm going for the gold," he told his teammates before climbing up the ladder. He no longer wanted to win just for himself. He wanted to win to prove that no one should be judged by the color of his or her skin.

For his final dive in the 10-meter platform event, Sammy decided to perform the forward three-and-a-half somersault. This was a very dangerous move. The slightest miscalculation in timing could lead to a serious, even fatal, injury.

Sammy faced a crowd of thousands. His mouth was dry. He heard the sound of water lapping against the sides of the pool, the murmuring of the people, the beating of his heart.

Never before had Sammy felt such intense pressure. He had trained sixteen years for this—a moment that would last barely sixteen seconds from the time he dived to when the scores would be revealed.

Sammy closed his eyes, and in his mind he was twelve years old again. It was Wednesday at the pool. He and Hart were practicing somersaults. Somehow, this image calmed Sammy's nerves. He opened his eyes, took a deep breath, and leaped off the edge of the platform.

Sammy flew through the air. He did one . . . then . . . two . . . then three . . . and a half somersaults!

The crowd gasped.

As Sammy surfaced, drops of water trickled over his eyes. He shook his head and blinked. Then he saw the scores.

    7.0
    9.0
    9.5
    9.5
    9.5
    9.5

And then . . . 10.0. Ten! He had a perfect score! Sammy Lee was an Olympic champion. ❖

✳ List three words that describe Sammy's personality.
What details from the selection support your thoughts?

Word that describes Sammy	Details from the selection that support your thoughts

✳ Now that you've read the selection, what do you think
the author wants you to understand from the title?

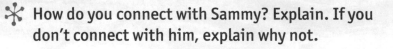

✳ How do you connect with Sammy? Explain. If you don't connect with him, explain why not.

....

....

....

....

....

....

....

....

....

....

....

....

Connecting with a real person can help you better understand his or her life experiences.

5 LESSON

When you make connections with a character's thoughts and ideas, you learn about both the character and yourself.

In this chapter from the short novel *Julian, Dream Doctor,* Julian daydreams about surprising his dad with a birthday gift. As you read, underline sentences and phrases from Julian's thoughts that connect with your own. Write about your connections in the **Response Notes**.

from Julian, Dream Doctor
by Ann Cameron

Every year we have a birthday party for my dad. Every year, the week before his birthday, my mom, Huey, and I go out and buy him a present.

This year was no different.

We went out. We got Dad a really good bowling ball. We wrapped it up and hid it in the back of the closet.

But then I started thinking. It would be nice to do something special for my dad. It would be nice to give him a surprise party and, besides the bowling ball, one special gift—something he had always dreamed of.

Once I thought of it, I could even imagine it happening. I could see myself showing Dad a mysterious box with a big bow on it, and Dad opening it and saying, "But Julian, nobody—nobody ever knew! This is what I've always dreamed of! Julian, you're a genius! This is the most unforgettable birthday that I have ever had!"

And then he would give me a big hug and be so excited he would lift me way off the ground.

Response Notes

I could imagine it so clearly that it seemed like it had already happened. I could see my mom being surprised too and saying, "Julian, how did you ever know what Dad wanted? You must have read his mind!"

The only thing I couldn't imagine was what was in the box. What did Dad dream of? What did he like more than anything? I didn't know.

I wanted to tell my best friend, Gloria, about my idea, but she was on vacation. So I told my little brother, Huey. I got Huey to practice asking Dad questions so we could find out his secret dream. ❖

✳ How do you connect with Julian's daydream? Explain.

✳ What are some good questions that Huey could ask Dad to figure out Dad's secret dream?

1. ....
....

2. ....
....

3. ....
....

4. ....
....

✳ Think of a close friend or family member. What kind of surprise party would you like to throw for him or her? How could you find out what special gift the person wanted most?

....
....
....
....
....
....
....

✳ **What special gift do you wish for? Draw it.**

Making connections with thoughts and ideas in a story will help you understand the story and yourself.

The words that characters say to each other are called **dialogue.** By making connections with dialogue, you can better understand how a character's feelings and experiences are similar to and different from your own.

In this folktale, the knee-high man searches for the key to his dream. As you read, underline sentences in the dialogue that connect with your thoughts or experiences. Write about your connections in the **Response Notes.**

The Knee-High Man by Julius Lester

Once upon a time there was a knee-high man. He was no taller than a person's knees. Because he was so short, he was very unhappy. He wanted to be big like everybody else.

One day he decided to ask the biggest animal he could find how he could get big. So he went to see Mr. Horse. "Mr. Horse, how can I get big like you?"

Mr. Horse said, "Well, eat a whole lot of corn. Then run around a lot. After a while you'll be as big as me."

The knee-high man did just that. He ate so much corn that his stomach hurt. Then he ran and ran and ran until his legs hurt. But he didn't get any bigger. So he decided that Mr. Horse had told him something wrong. He decided to go ask Mr. Bull.

"Mr. Bull? How can I get big like you?"

Mr. Bull said, "Eat a whole lot of grass. Then bellow and bellow as loud as you can. The first thing you know, you'll be as big as me."

So the knee-high man ate a whole field of grass. That made his stomach hurt. He bellowed and bellowed and bellowed all day and all night. That made his throat hurt. But he didn't get any bigger. So he decided that Mr. Bull was wrong too.

Response Notes

Now he didn't know anyone else to ask. One night he heard Mr. Hoot Owl hooting, and he remembered that Mr. Owl knew everything. "Mr. Owl? How can I get big like Mr. Horse and Mr. Bull?"

"What do you want to be big for?" Mr. Hoot Owl asked.

"I want to be big so that when I get into a fight, I can whip everybody," the knee-high man said.

Mr. Hoot Owl hooted. "Anybody ever try to pick a fight with you?"

The knee-high man thought a minute. "Well, now that you mention it, nobody ever did try to start a fight with me."

Mr. Owl said, "Well, you don't have any reason to fight. Therefore, you don't have any reason to be bigger than you are."

"But, Mr. Owl," the knee-high man said, "I want to be big so I can see far into the distance."

Mr. Hoot Owl hooted. "If you climb a tall tree, you can see into the distance from the top."

The knee-high man was quiet for a minute. "Well, I hadn't thought of that."

Mr. Hoot Owl hooted again. "And that's what's wrong, Mr. Knee-High Man. You hadn't done any thinking at all. I'm smaller than you, and you don't see me worrying about being big. Mr. Knee-High Man, you wanted something that you didn't need." ❖

✳ What do you learn about Mr. Knee-High Man from his dialogues with other characters?

....

....

....

....

....

✳ What have you tried to change about yourself? Did it work? Explain.

....

....

....

....

....

....

....

....

Making connections with dialogue will help you understand a character's thoughts and feelings.

✳ How does each selection from this unit connect with the theme of "follow your dreams"? Write your thoughts in the chart.

Title	How does each selection connect with the theme of "follow your dreams"?
"Dreams"	
Uncle Jed's Barbershop	
Sixteen Years in Sixteen Seconds	
Julian, Dream Doctor	
"The Knee-High Man"	

Asking Questions

Imagine that you're a detective. You get called to a crime scene where you see a boy and a girl pointing to a broken lock on an empty bike rack. What's the first thing you do? You ask: What happened? What did you see? Who did you see?

Reading is like detective work, too. You discover clues and ask questions to make sense of the text. **Asking questions** helps you recognize what you already know about a topic and what more you would like to know.

In this unit, you'll read about adults and children who make **change** in the world around them. You'll ask questions and discover clues to better understand their lives and actions.

QUESTIONS ABOUT CHARACTERS

Thinking about characters' words and actions can help you better understand the decisions they make. As you read, **ask questions** about what the characters say and do. Your thoughts about these questions will help you understand the text.

As you read this excerpt from the novel *Frindle*, notice what Nick, John, and Mrs. Granger say and do. Underline text that raises questions for you about the characters. Write your questions in the **Response Notes**.

Response Notes

What's a frindle?
Why does Nick use that strange word?

from **Frindle** by Andrew Clements

School was the perfect place to launch a new word, and since this was a major historical event, Nick wanted it to begin in exactly the right class—seventh-period language arts.

<u>Nick raised his hand first thing after the bell rang and said, "Mrs. Granger, I forgot my frindle."</u>

Sitting three rows away, John blurted out, "I have an extra one you can borrow, Nick."

Then John made a big show of looking for something in his backpack. "I think I have an extra frindle, I mean, I told my mom to get me three or four. I'm sure I had an extra frindle in here yesterday, but I must have taken it . . . wait . . . oh yeah, here it is."

And then, John made a big show of throwing it over to Nick, and Nick missed it on purpose.

Then he made a big show of finding it.

Mrs. Granger and every kid in the class got the message loud and clear. That black plastic thing that Nick borrowed from John had a funny name . . . a different name . . . a new name—*frindle*.

There was a lot of giggling, but Mrs. Granger turned up the power in her eyes and swept the room into silence. And the rest of the class went by according to plan—her plan.

As everyone was leaving after class, Mrs. Granger said, "Nicholas? I'd like to have . . . a word with you," and she emphasized the word *word*.

Nick's mouth felt dry, and he gulped, but his mind stayed clear. He walked up to her desk. "Yes, Mrs. Granger?"

"It's a funny idea, Nicholas, but I will not have my class disrupted again. Is that clear?" Her eyes were lit up, but it was mostly light, not much heat.

"Idea? What idea?" asked Nick, and he tried to make his eyes as blank as possible.

"You know what I mean, Nicholas. I am talking about the performance that you and John gave at the start of class. I am talking about—this," and she held up her pen, an old maroon fountain pen with a blue cap.

"But I really didn't have a frindle with me," said Nick, amazed at his own bravery. And hiding behind his glasses, Nick kept his eyes wide and blank.

Mrs. Granger's eyes flashed, and then narrowed, and her lips formed a thin, hard line. She was quiet for a few seconds, and then she said, "I see. Very well. Then I guess we have nothing more to discuss today, Nicholas. You may go."

"Thanks, Mrs. Granger," said Nick, and he grabbed his backpack and headed for the door. And when he was just stepping into the hallway, he said, "And I promise I won't ever forget my frindle again. Bye." ❖

Is Mrs. Granger *mad*, or does she think it's funny?

MATH HOMEWORK
13 – 203
EVEN ?'s

HISTOR
W

✳ What questions arose as you read the selection? What do your questions tell you about Nick and Mrs. Granger?

Nick

Character's words or actions:
"I forgot my frindle."
Question raised:
Why does Nick use this word?
What does your question tell you about the character?
Maybe Nick wants to make a new word.

Mrs. Granger

Character's words or actions:
Question raised:
What does your question tell you about the character?

Nick or Mrs. Granger

Character's words or actions:
Question raised:
What does your question tell you about the character?

✳ **What kind of change is Nick trying to make?**
What do you think he's trying to accomplish?

....

....

....

....

....

....

....

Asking questions about
characters helps you better
understand their decisions
and actions.

In the 1950s in much of the South, African Americans were not given the same rights as whites. Blacks were forced to go to separate schools, eat in separate restaurants, and sit in separate parts of theaters and buses. On December 1, 1955, in Montgomery, Alabama, Rosa Parks refused to sit in the back of a bus. Her courage set off many changes.

As you read this poem about Rosa Parks, think about the big ideas the poet wants you to understand. Stop after every two **stanzas** and ask yourself: what does the author want me to understand from the details? Write your thoughts in the **Response Notes**. Underline details that hint at the big ideas.

Response Notes

The Many and the Few
by J. Patrick Lewis

It was an Alabama day
For the Many and the Few.
There wasn't really much to do;
No one had very much to say

Until a bus, the 4:15,
Drove by. But no one chanced to see
It stop to pick up history.
The doors closed slowly on a scene:

The quiet seamstress paid her fare
And took the one seat she could find,
And, as it happened, just behind
The Many People sitting there.

The Many People paid no mind
Until the driver, J. P. Blake,
Told the Few of *them* to take
The deeper seats. But she declined.

Blake stopped the bus and called the police;
And Many a fire was set that night,
And Many a head turned ghostly white
Because she dared disturb the peace.

To celebrate the ride that marks
The debt the Many owe the Few,
One day of freedom grew into
The Century of Rosa Parks. ❖

❋ Who are the Many in the poem? Who are the Few?

✳ What are some big ideas from the poem? Share and discuss your ideas with a partner. Write your ideas in the chart. If your partner's ideas are different from yours, do they still make sense to you?

My big ideas	My partner's big ideas

Rosa Parks Highway

No Standing Allowed

✳ Write about one new thought that you and your partner discussed.

....

....

....

....

....

Asking questions about details will help you better understand the big ideas in a text.

Like Rosa Parks, Ruby Bridges lived in the South during the time of segregation. During this time, African American children were not allowed to go to school with white children in the South. In 1960, a law was passed that made it illegal to have separate schools for white and black students. Ruby Bridges was the first African American student to go to an all-white school in the South. Her first day there changed the history of civil rights in the United States.

As you read this passage from Ruby Bridges' **autobiography**, ask questions about the text. Asking questions will help you better understand the selection. Write your questions in the **Response Notes**. Underline any sentences that help you find the answers.

from Through My Eyes By Ruby Bridges

November 14, 1960

My mother took special care getting me ready for school. When somebody knocked on my door that morning, my mother expected to see people from the NAACP. Instead, she saw four serious-looking white men, dressed in suits and wearing armbands. They were U.S. federal marshals. They had come to drive us to school and stay with us all day. I learned later they were carrying guns.

I remember climbing into the back seat of the marshals' car with my mother, but I don't remember feeling frightened. William Frantz Public School was only five blocks away, so one of the marshals in the front seat told my mother right away what we should do when we got there.

"Let us get out of the car first," the marshal said. "Then you'll get out, and the four of us will surround you and your daughter. We'll walk up to the door together. Just walk straight ahead, and don't look back."

Response Notes

Response Notes

When we were near the school, my mother said, "Ruby, I want you to behave yourself today and do what the marshals say."

We drove down North Galvez Street to the point where it crosses Alvar. I remember looking out of the car as we pulled up to the Frantz school. There were barricades and people shouting and policemen everywhere. I thought maybe it was Mardi Gras, the carnival that takes place in New Orleans every year. Mardi Gras was always noisy.

As we walked through the crowd, I didn't see any faces. I guess that's because I wasn't very tall and I was surrounded by the marshals. People yelled and threw things. I could see the school building, and it looked bigger and nicer than my old school. When we climbed the high steps to the front door, there were policemen in uniforms at the top. The policemen at the door and the crowd behind us made me think this was an important place.

It must be college, I thought to myself.

✳ What are the big ideas so far?

Once we were inside the building, the marshals walked us up a flight of stairs. The school office was at the top. My mother and I went in and were told to sit in the principal's office. The marshals sat outside. There were windows in the room where we waited. That meant everybody passing by could see us. I remember noticing everyone was white.

All day long, white parents rushed into the office. They were upset. They were arguing and pointing at us. When they took their children to school that morning, the parents hadn't been sure whether William Frantz would be integrated that day or not. After my mother and I arrived, they ran into classrooms and dragged their children out of the school. From behind the windows in the office, all I saw was confusion. I told myself that this must be the way it is in a big school.

That whole first day, my mother and I just sat and waited. We didn't talk to anybody. I remember watching a big, round clock on the wall. When it was 3:00 and time to go home, I was glad. I had thought my new school would be hard, but the first day was easy. ✤

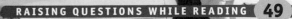

How do you think Ruby felt that first day? Write a diary entry from Ruby's point of view. Tell about her thoughts and feelings.

✳ What questions do you still have about Ruby Bridges or the time in which she lived? Discuss your questions with a partner.

....

....

....

....

✳ How does asking questions keep you interested in your reading?

....

....

....

....

....

....

✳ What do Rosa Parks, Ruby Bridges, and Nick from *Frindle* have in common?

....

....

....

....

Asking questions while reading will help you better understand and remember a text.

QUESTIONS ABOUT CHARACTERS' DECISIONS

The decisions you make can tell a lot about you. What you decide to eat, to play, and to read are clues about who you are. The decisions a character makes tell about him or her, too. You can **question a character's decision** to learn about him or her. You might ask:

- Why does the character make that decision?
- What does the decision tell you about the character?

As you read this passage from the novel *A Dog Called Kitty*, think about the decision Dad makes and how it changes the family. In the **Response Notes**, write questions about his decision. Underline information in the story that helps you answer your questions.

Response Notes

from A Dog Called Kitty by Bill Wallace

Probably the only thing that saved me from listening to car horns and breathing the funny smelling air that hangs over St. Louis like a thick brown cloud was Dad's dream.

Far back as I could remember, Dad was talking about a farm. About how he used to visit his grandparents in the country. And he had this dream about some day moving from the big city and getting a farm all his own.

Mama—she said he was just dreaming. When Dad would get to talking about it too much, she'd remind him of that fact. Always say something about how he didn't know the first thing about farming. How he couldn't leave a good job like he had and all sorts of stuff.

Then, lo and behold, we woke up one morning and found Dad wasn't dreaming anymore.

There was this big moving van parked in front of our apartment. When Mama said something about the neighbors upstairs must be leaving, Dad only smiled

and went to open the front door. Mama got downright *upset* when the men started hauling her furniture away. That's when Dad showed her the deed to a house and 160 acres of land in Oklahoma. Mama didn't do anything but stand and stare at him for a long, long time. Then, she got real pale and sickly looking. And when she commenced crying and laughing—both at the same time—that's when Dad told me and Chuckie to go outside and play. Even out there, we could hear the fussin' and arguin' that came from our place. All the other folks in our end of the apartment complex must have heard it, too. 'Cause they kept looking out their windows or coming out on the sidewalk to see what was going on. Mom and Dad went right on yelling and fussin' until the men from the moving company had everything hauled out and were waiting in their truck.

At last, Dad opened the front door and started down the steps. He stopped and looked back at Mama. Then, in a real soft voice, he said, "I love you more than you'll ever know, Helen. My life wouldn't be much without you." Then, his face got real stern looking. "But me and my sons are moving to that farm in Oklahoma. We want you to come. We need you with us. But, with or without you—I've made up my mind."

I don't remember being so scared about anything as when Dad said that. He marched me and Chuckie to the car. We got in the back, and he got in front. Started the engine.

I was about to cry. I told him I didn't want to go any place without Mama—only he didn't answer me.

Chuckie didn't help me much. He was busy chewing on his toy car and picking his nose. I guess he didn't say anything 'cause he was too little to know how much trouble our family was in.

Dad put the car in gear. My heart almost jumped up in my throat when he started to drive away.

It was about then Mama came trotting out the front door. She had her purse on her arm. Jumping on one foot trying to pull on her shoes. Dad stopped the car. She got in.

But it was clean into the next day before Mama said one single word. Then it was only to tell Dad she needed to stop at a filling station to go to the bathroom. ❖

※ Look back at your Response Notes. Write one of your questions about Dad's decision. If you found an answer in the text, write what you found. If not, write what you think the answer might be. Then explain what your thoughts tell you about Dad.

Dad's decision:
My question about his decision:
My answer or thoughts:
What I learned about Dad:

✳ Now think about Mama's reaction. What questions do you have about it? What do your questions and thoughts teach you about Mama?

Mama's reaction:

My question about her reaction:

My answer or thoughts:

What I learned about Mama:

✳ Think about an important decision you have made. How did the decision affect you and others?

✳ **Imagine that you are Mama. Write a letter to Dad explaining why you're not talking to him.**

Dear Dad,

Signed,

Mama

Questioning the decisions that a character makes gives you clues about the character's personality.

5 LESSON

In most fiction stories, the characters face a problem. This problem is called the **conflict**. You can learn a lot about characters by studying how they react to the conflict.

As you read the second passage from *A Dog Called Kitty*, think about the conflict the characters face. Notice what happens, why it happens, and what it tells you about the characters.

As you read, underline words and phrases that show the conflict between the characters. In the **Response Notes**, write questions you have about the conflict.

from A Dog Called Kitty by Bill Wallace

Response Notes

Her mad spell lasted almost two weeks. We had moved into our new house and had things pretty well settled—everything except Mom and Dad, that is. Mama was still pouting. Not talking to Dad. She even slept in the bedroom with Chuckie at night.

Anyway, it was Chuckie who finally snapped her out of her orneriness. She was getting him ready for his bath one night, and I guess he'd finally noticed that things weren't running quite as smooth as they usually did. I was sitting in the living room watching TV with Dad when he came racing in.

He was stark-naked and red as a lobster from the top of his head clean down to his bellybutton. (When he got mad, Chuckie held his breath until he was about to pop, but I don't ever remember him being as red as he was that night.)

Chuckie marched up in front of Dad. He squared off and kicked him right on the shins.

Dad sorta jumped, not quite knowing why Chuckie had kicked him, and not quite being able to figure out why he was naked as a jaybird and red all over.

Finally, Chuckie opened his mouth and let out all his air. Then, he scrunched his little round face up till he was real mean and angry looking.

"I don't know why Mommy's so mad at you. But I'm mad, too. My Daddy's a mean, mean old toot!"

I guess Dad had been real worried about Mama not liking our new home, and so upset about the way she'd been treating him lately, he was ready to pop.

And that's just what he did. He started laughing so hard the whole room seemed to shake. His belly bounced up and down and tears leaked from his eyes.

Mama had been watching from the door of Chuckie's bedroom. It wasn't any time before she was doubled over laughing, too. Directly, she came into the living room and sat down on Dad's lap.

All that laughing only made Chuckie mad. He stood there in front of them and turned red, all over.

That only made Mama and Dad laugh harder.

I didn't know what they were laughing so hard about but, after watching Chuckie for a while, I got to laughing, too.

Finally, Mama scooped Chuckie up in her arms and snuggled him up real tight. Dad waved for me to come over and sit on the arm of his chair. All four of us sat there, and Mama told us why she'd been so upset about leaving everything to move to a farm in Oklahoma. But she said she'd decided it wasn't such a bad place after all, that she was glad we were together and happy again, and that she wasn't mad at Dad anymore, and we shouldn't be, either. ❖

✳ Look back at the selection and the questions you
   wrote in the Response Notes. Use your answers to fill
   in the chart.

Mama

What does the conflict tell you about Mama?

Dad

What does the conflict tell you about Dad?

Chuckie

What does the conflict tell you about Chuckie?

Narrator

What does the conflict tell you about the narrator?

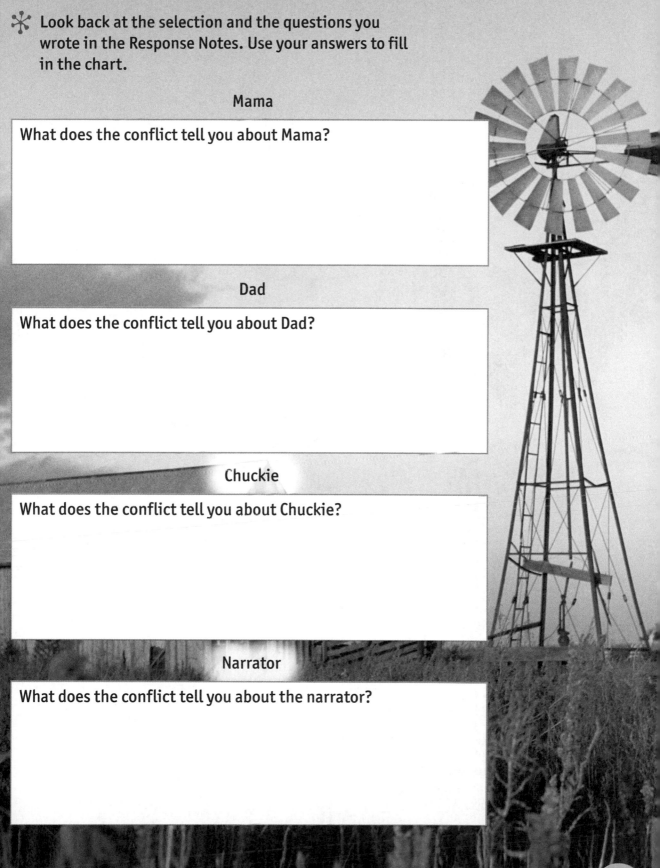

✳ How does Chuckie resolve the conflict?

....

....

....

....

....

....

....

....

✳ Write about a time when you were as angry as Mama.
   How did it get resolved?

....

....

....

....

....

....

....

....

Asking questions
about the conflict will
help you better understand
the characters.

Have you ever taken a picture with a digital camera? If so, you know how easy it is. Just point, click, and there's your photo. Taking pictures wasn't always that easy, though.

In this passage from *Children of the Wild West*, a nonfiction book, you'll read about the early days of photography. You might discover new facts about photography or about the Wild West. **Asking questions** will help you make better sense of the new information.

As you read, underline new facts you learn. In the **Response Notes**, write questions about the facts.

from Children of the Wild West
by Russell Freedman

On May 19, 1841, a dozen covered wagons and seventy men, women, and children left Missouri and headed for the Pacific Coast. They were the first pioneers to travel west by wagon train. It is doubtful that any of these people had ever seen a photograph.

Photography was a new invention. The earliest photographs had been displayed for the first time in France just two years before, in the summer of 1839.

The growth of photography and the opening of the American West took place at the same time. By the 1850s, frontier photographers were traveling throughout the West. Their cameras were big and bulky. Their equipment was often crude. Even so, they were able to picture the frontier as the pioneers actually saw it.

In those days, simple rolls of film were unknown. Instead, photographers used large glass plate negatives that were messy and hard to handle. Just before a picture was taken, the glass plate was coated with sticky chemicals. It had to be placed in the camera and exposed right away, while it was still moist. Then the plate had to be removed from the camera and developed on the spot, before the chemicals dried. A photographer's covered wagon served as his darkroom. Wherever he went, he had to haul with him hundreds of pounds of photographic equipment.

The first cameras could not capture motion. Because of the long exposure time needed, the camera had to be placed securely on a tripod. The people being photographed had to stand or sit absolutely still. If anyone moved, the picture would be blurred.

A frontier photographer might take more than an hour to assemble a group for a portrait, prepare the glass negative, take the picture, and then develop the negative. Yet people were eager to pose in front of the camera. Some of them would have their picture taken only once in their lives. ❖

✳ How are today's cameras similar to and different from early cameras? Write your thoughts in the Venn diagram.

Cameras today

Early cameras

✳ What does the author want you to understand about early cameras?

....

....

....

....

....

....

✳ How does pausing and asking questions help you improve your understanding of a text?

....

....

....

....

....

....

....

Asking questions about new information will help you better understand it.

Determining Importance

It's the beginning of the school year. You want to join the soccer team, take trumpet lessons, help your brother build a shed, and rake leaves to earn extra money. And then there's homework. You can't do them all, so how will you decide which activities to do? You'll have to decide which are the most important to you.

When you read, you make decisions about what's important, too. You base your decisions on what matters to you most, what you want to remember, and what you think the author wants you to know.

The selections in this unit show different ways people and animals try to **maintain balance** in the world around them. As you read, you will become more aware of how your mind **determines the importance of ideas** in a text.

Do you have a favorite character from a story or movie? What do you like about him or her? A character's thoughts, words, and actions can tell you **important ideas** about the character and about life in general. Thinking about a character can help you better understand a text.

In this excerpt from the short story "Apple Blossoms," Jason tries to maintain balance as he recites a poem in front of the class. As you read, underline text that shows important ideas about Jason. In the **Response Notes**, write why they're important.

Response Notes

The narrator likes to make people laugh.

He's nervous!

from Apple Blossoms by Terry Trueman

I make my way to the front of the room. <u>The same kids who laugh at everything I say, laugh at the way I'm walking, so I break into a gorilla walk, swinging my arms down and leaning way over from one side to the other, then back again.</u> Even more kids laugh. Ms. Souza doesn't laugh, though, so I stop messing around and try to get serious as I stand in front of the class.

I want to get a good grade on this, but I'm feeling weird. My palms are sweaty, and there are little trickles of sweat under my arms. My hands aren't shaking, like Fred Gritten's were, but I feel tight in my throat, like I should cough or something. Suddenly I think to myself, I wish I'd practiced reading my poem out loud. Too late now, but I wish I had.

I put my sheet of paper onto the podium thing, and I put my hands on the side of it. <u>My palms are so sweaty that I'm sure my hands will leave little wet spots, but I try not to think about that.</u>

I look out at everybody. Their stares, their expressions, make me feel even more scared. Are they expecting me to joke around, even though they know I'll get killed if I do? I realize now that I don't really know what my poem is even about. I mean, I know the springtime and the war and that the first line is something about guys marching and stuff.

I'm feeling more and more nervous, looking out at everybody. A couple more kids, plus the first kids who laughed earlier, start to smile.

Ms. Souza asks, "Are you ready, Jason?"

More giggling from the troops.

"Sure," I say.

I think to myself, The heck with oral interpretation, I'm just gonna read this kind of slow and pretend I understand it and get it over with. It's only eight lines long.

✳ What important ideas have you learned about Jason so far?

I start to read the poem and I get through the first line. I have no idea what I've just said. It's like there's a battle raging all around me and inside me. My nerves are racing and exploding. I can't think straight. I start to read the second line and now I hear myself. It's about the soldiers in springtime and they're marching along and the poem says what they can smell . . .

"The scent of assel bloppems fills the air . . . "

I freeze.

What did I just say?

Did I just say *assel bloppems*?

What's an assel bloppem?

There's a soft, horrible gasp from the class. Now the room is deadly quiet. I keep staring at the page; eight short lines, it begins to swirl.

What did I say?

Where am I?

I find my way back to the start of the line and try again. "The scent of . . ." I hesitate for half a second, I can do this, I can say this . . . but it's so quiet, so tense . . .

"The scent of . . . assel bloppems . . ."

The roar of the class laughing drowns out the rest of my words.

"What?" I mumble. "What'd I say? What'd I say?"

Nobody answers, I'm not even sure they can hear me through all their laughter. In all the clowning I've ever done, all the times I've tried to make kids laugh, I've never heard laughter as loud or long or real as this before. But when I look up at Ms. Souza, she isn't smiling. Fred isn't laughing either; his expression is worried, like he wishes he could rescue me.

My face goes bright red; I can feel it. Now sweat is pouring down from my armpits like somebody turned on a faucet.

Without knowing I'm going to say it, I blurt out "Assel bloppems" again.

Everybody roars even louder. Their laughter becomes explosions, bombs going off, bullets and shrapnel flying all around my ears. Kids are doubled over, almost falling out of their chairs, they're laughing so hard. My head is dizzy. My vision blurs. I can't see the words of the poem anymore; I can barely even see the page.

Finally Ms. Souza says, "That's enough, Jason. You can sit down." ❖

✳ What important ideas do you learn about Jason from his poetry reading? Fill in the chart with your thoughts.

Important ideas I learn about Jason	Details that support my thoughts
He is nervous.	His palms are sweaty and his throat is tight.

✳ **What important ideas do you learn from Jason and his experience? Fill in the chart with your thoughts.**

Important ideas I learn from Jason	Details that support my thoughts
It's important to practice.	He wishes he had practiced more.

✳ **Discuss your charts with a partner. List one new idea that you discovered from your discussion.**

....

....

....

....

....

....

....

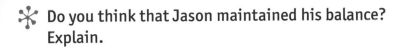

✳ Do you think that Jason maintained his balance?
Explain.

....

....

....

....

....

....

✳ How do you feel about speaking in front of the class?

....

....

....

....

....

....

Look for important ideas
in a character's thoughts,
words, and actions.

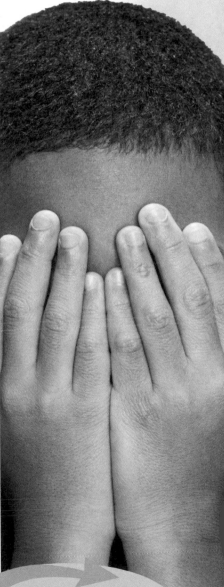

Authors of nonfiction include a lot of information in the texts they write. They often organize the information in **text features**, such as headings, diagrams, and charts. These text features help you decide and remember which ideas are most important.

As you read this field guide entry on Snowy Owls, notice the text features that the author includes. Underline information that you think is important. In the **Response Notes**, write why it is important.

Response Notes

Snowy Owl
by Jonathan P. Latimer and Karen Stray Nolting

Most of the time Snowy Owls are found in the Far North, where their white feathers can provide camouflage in the snow. But every few years, they suddenly appear much farther south than usual. This is because their favorite prey, the lemming, has periodic declines in its population. The owls are unable to find enough food, so they move south where they can find rodents and other animals to eat.

The rise and fall of the number of lemmings also affects the nesting pattern of Snowy Owls. They nest and raise young in years when lemmings are plentiful. In years when lemmings are scarce, Snowy Owls raise fewer chicks or may not nest at all.

Snowy Owls are large and powerful. They hunt during the day and find their prey by sight and sound.

Lemming

- Male Snowy Owls will defend their nests against almost any intruder, including wolves and foxes. Females are known to pretend to have a broken wing to lure intruders away from the nest.

- Geese and ducks sometimes nest near Snowy Owl nests for protection against Arctic Foxes.

Habitat During winter Snowy Owls can be found in the North in open country, including prairies, fields, marshes, beaches, and dunes. In summer these owls move north to the Arctic tundra.

Voice Snowy Owls are usually silent, except during nesting season when they are known to make a loud, repeated *krow-ow* while flying. They also sometimes make a repeated call that sounds like *rick*.

Food Small rodents, especially lemmings, are the main food for Snowy Owls, but they also hunt larger animals such as squirrels, rabbits, opossums, and skunks. They also hunt birds—sometimes large birds such as ducks or geese—snakes, lizards, frogs, insects, and scorpions. ✢

✳ What are the four most important ideas you learned about Snowy Owls? Explain what helped you decide which ideas were important.

Important idea about Snowy Owls	What supports your decision?

✻ Compare your chart with a partner's chart. Are your ideas similar or different? Explain why you think your ideas are similar or different.

✻ How does the theme of "maintaining balance" connect with Snowy Owls?

Look for important ideas in text features. A text feature can be a heading, diagram, chart, or special print.

Authors of nonfiction organize their writing in different ways. The next selection you will read is organized around **problems and solutions**. When you notice how an author organizes information, you can more easily determine the important ideas.

In this excerpt from the nonfiction book *Forensics*, you'll read about how police officers look for clues at a crime scene. As you read each section, underline the main problem. In the **Response Notes**, write about the solution.

Response Notes

from Forensics by Richard Platt

The crime scene

Blue lights flash on a dark street. "Police line—do not cross" written on yellow plastic tape flaps between trees. Uniformed figures hold back a curious crowd. Welcome to a crime scene. Police officers and detectives take extra care to preserve crime scenes exactly as they find them—because evidence is fragile, and clumsy feet and prying hands can easily destroy it. Without evidence, it may be impossible to solve a crime and catch the criminals who carried it out.

One and only chance

The first police officers to arrive at the scene of a crime must take a careful look around but avoid disturbing anything that they find. There are very good reasons for this caution and care—the first officers to arrive have a special, once-only chance because they see the crime scene completely fresh and untouched. Very soon their own actions—and those of others—will make changes that can never be undone. For example, just walking across a carpet to help an injured person can destroy the footprints of a fleeing attacker.

Preserving evidence

Crime scene officers must take quick steps to protect and preserve the crime scene. They try to see where criminals could have entered before committing the crime—and how they left afterward. These places may hold important clues, such as the suspect's fingerprints, so it is vital that they remain untouched. Crime scene officers also try to guess where they will *not* find evidence. They will only use these areas to enter and leave the crime scene so that they do not disturb other, more important places.

Securing the scene

Once the crime scene is taped off, there are other simple but essential precautions that officers need to take. They must not eat, drink, or smoke because these activities leave traces that may later confuse investigators. For the same reason, they must not use the telephone or the bathroom if they are part of the crime scene. Sometimes their work forces them to make a change to the crime scene—such as opening a door to enter. If this happens, they make a written note recording that the door was shut when they arrived. Details like this can make the difference between a criminal going to jail and escaping unpunished.

Vital witnesses

For all their careful observation and note taking, officers can never know as much about a crime as someone who actually saw it happen. These witnesses are vital to an investigation. Police race to identify them and make sure that they do not leave the crime scene before being interviewed. ❖

POLICE LINE DO NOT CROSS

✳ Look over the selection. Think about the problem and solution in each section. What important ideas do you learn from each problem and solution? Fill in the chart with your thoughts.

Section heading	Important ideas you learn
"One and only chance"	
"Preserving evidence"	
"Securing the scene"	
"Vital witnesses"	

Studying a problem and how it's solved can help you determine important ideas.

✳ How does focusing on the problems and solutions help you find important ideas?

....

....

....

....

....

....

✳ Reread one of the first three selections in this unit. Did your thoughts change this time about which ideas were most important? Don't forget to list which selection you reread.

Selection title: ....

New thoughts about important ideas: ....

....

....

....

....

....

....

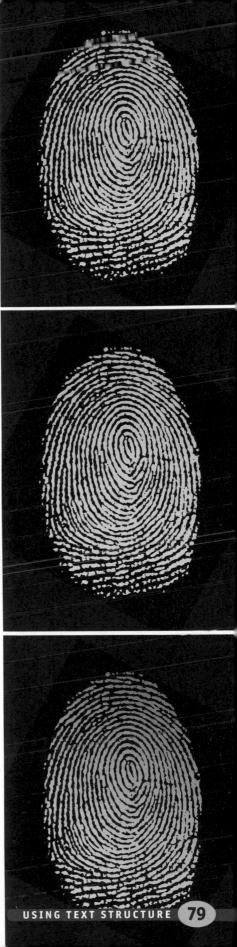

When you read nonfiction, you often learn new facts. Thinking about new facts can lead you to new understandings, or big ideas about the world.

This selection is about cheetahs. They are now an endangered species. As you read, underline important ideas you find. In the **Response Notes**, write about why they are important.

Response Notes

from Caring for Cheetahs
by Rosanna Hansen

When a wild cheetah starts a hunt, it often climbs a tree or even a tall termite mound. From there, the cheetah scans the plains until it spots a likely target— a small antelope on the edge of its herd, perhaps. The cheetah starts to creep as close as possible to the antelope. Suddenly, the cheetah bursts out of its hiding place and races toward its prey. By the time the antelope leaps away in a panic, the cheetah has already closed in. If the cheetah catches the antelope, it will drag its prey to the ground and kill it. But the cheetah is successful in its hunts only about half the time. The rest of the time, the prey outlasts the cheetah and gets away, then the cheetah goes hungry.

Meat eaters like cheetahs are an important part of their ecosystems and food chains. By hunting the weak, sick, or slow members of an antelope herd, a cheetah helps to keep the herd healthy and strong. Also, cheetahs are partly responsible for maintaining a balance between the number of prey animals and the amount of plant food available for them to eat. Without predators like the cheetah, the herds of prey animals might get too large. When there are too many prey animals, there is not enough plant food to go around. Then the herd animals may get weak and start to starve.

Cheetahs can be found in many parts of Africa, but Namibia is considered the cheetah capital of the world. More than 3,000 wild cheetahs live there.

AFRICA

Namibia

ATLANTIC OCEAN

BUILT FOR THE CHASE

A cheetah's body is an elegant running machine. Cheetah's have:

- **A long, flexible spine**
  The cheetah's backbone acts like a giant spring, coiling and uncoiling as the cheetah runs.

- **Long, thin legs and claws that grip firmly**
  The cheetah's long, blunt claws act like the spikes on track shoes. The spikes keep the cheetah from skidding when it sprints.

- **A small, sleek head with large nostrils**
  The cheetah's big nostrils help it inhale and exhale huge quantities of air while it runs, supplying its body with oxygen and getting rid of carbon dioxide.

- **Large eyes and keen eyesight**
  The cheetah can see for long distances and detect tiny movements in the brush. Also, the black "teardrop" marks running down from a cheetah's eyes may reduce glare from the sun, like the black smudges that football players wear under their eyes.

- **A long, muscular tail**
  A cheetah's tail acts like a counterweight, keeping the cheetah on course as it whips around curves at scorching speed. ✤

✳ What important ideas did you learn about cheetahs and the food chain?

....

....

....

✳ What new understandings did you develop about the food chain and animals in general?

....

....

....

✳ The author of *Caring for Cheetahs* feels strongly about preserving cheetahs in the wild. Think of an issue about which you feel strongly. What is the issue? Write your thoughts and feelings about it.

I feel strongly about

....

....

....

....

....

✳ Think about the issue you wrote about on page 82.
Design a poster that explains your position.

Important ideas from a selection can lead you to important ideas beyond the selection.

When you learn new facts about a topic, you often **change your beliefs** about what's important about the topic.

What do you know about bats? Are they just scary-looking flying mammals? Do they help people in any way? As you read this informational piece about bats, underline facts that are new to you. In the **Response Notes**, write comments or questions about the new information.

Before you begin, make a list of what you already know about bats.

What I know about bats:

....

....

....

....

....

Three Cheers for Bats!
by Laurence Pringle

To many people, bats are scary, ugly creatures. The superstitions about them range from tales of Dracula-type vampires to the belief that they entangle themselves in people's hair. These notions about bats are still common; no wonder bats are still feared and persecuted in many lands.

These old beliefs are disappearing, however, as people learn about the lives of *real* bats. About a thousand kinds of bats live on all continents except Antarctica. None are blind, and some see very well. Large fruit-eating bats that live in the tropics have big eyes and doglike snouts. They're called flying foxes.

Most bats are insect eaters, and they are the ones with weird faces. They usually have big ears and sometimes have odd-looking noses. With their beady little eyes they see as well as mice or other small mammals. To catch food in the dark, though, they rely on a sonar, or echolocation, system that is more advanced than anything devised by people. In fact, scientists still don't understand many details of this extraordinary system.

The bats emit high-pitched squeaks that we cannot hear. Some of these sounds echo off objects in front of the flying bats: tree branches, wires, flying insects. Bats listen to the echoes and get an instantaneous and changing picture in their brains of what lies ahead. They dodge twigs and other obstacles. They zoom in on moths and even tiny mosquitoes.

The odd-looking noses and ears of some bats are part of their sonar equipment. Their echolocation system works beautifully. Bats can and do easily avoid getting tangled in a person's hair. When they sometimes swoop near people who are outdoors at night, they are often chasing mosquitoes, which they pluck out of the air before the insects can feast on the humans.

Where mosquitoes are abundant, a small bat can catch several hundred in an hour. People who know this take steps to encourage bats to live near their home. They put up specially designed bat houses in which bats can rest in the daytime.

Bats can eat an astonishing number of flying insects. In Austin, Texas, a colony of nearly a million free-tailed bats consumes from fifteen to thirty thousand pounds of insects each summer night. People in the Austin area are proud of their bats and celebrate their return each summer.

✳ **What new information have you learned so far?**

....

....

....

....

Response Notes

Farther west, long-nosed bats feed on nectar within cactus flowers. The cacti, including the giant saguaro, bloom only at night. As the bats fly from one flower to another, dipping their noses deep inside, they also carry pollen from flower to flower. Without long-nosed bats, saguaros and other large cacti could not produce seeds.

In East Africa, the giant baobab tree is pollinated by bats. Its large white flowers open at night, an invitation to nectar-feeding bats. The baobab is called the "tree of life" because so many other plants and animals depend on it for their survival. Without bats, however, baobabs themselves would eventually die out. For the baobab, bats are the "mammals of life."

In tropical rain forests, flying foxes and other bats also are important pollinators. Fruit-eating bats play another vital role: Seeds from the fruit pass quickly through their digestive tracts and are expelled in flight. In this way, tree seeds are scattered in rain forests. When fruit bats fly over cleared land where agriculture has been abandoned, the seeds they drop make forest regrowth possible.

As the vital roles of bats in nature become better known, more and more people work to protect these creatures. Bats often rest or raise their young in caves or other shelters where they can easily be found and destroyed. In the United States, some bat colonies are now protected from disturbance. Metal gates have been built across the openings to their cave homes. People are kept out, and the bats can fly freely in and out.

Bats are intelligent and gentle. Their fur feels wonderfully soft to the touch. When people see a bat, they are often tempted to pick it up. This is not wise. Bats naturally hide in the daytime, and any bat that is not hidden may be sick. It may be dying of a disease called rabies that can be transmitted to humans through a bite. Never touch a bat that seems sick or injured.

If we leave bats alone, and leave their caves and other homes alone, they will thrive and continue to be some of the most fascinating and beneficial mammals on Earth. Hurrah for bats! ❖

✳ What new information did you learn about bats?

✳ How have your ideas about bats changed? Explain.

✳ Why do you think some people are afraid of bats?

....

....

....

....

....

✳ Imagine that you are a scientist who studies bats. You've been asked to write a short speech to help people understand the truth about bats. What information is most important? Write a short speech below.

....

....

....

....

....

....

....

Learning new information can change your beliefs about what is important.

....

....

6 LESSON

Poems about nature often include facts that explain the natural world. As you read this poem about a caterpillar, underline important facts that tell you about nature. In the **Response Notes**, write about why the facts are important.

Making Scents by Leslie Bulion

It isn't
that the skipper caterpillar
wants
his leaf house
that he skillfully strings together
with sticky silk,
to stay spotless
and tidy.

It isn't
that the skipper caterpillar
wants
every bit of the space
in his leafy homemade hideaway
all for his apple-green-striped wriggly
self.

The reason
that the skipper caterpillar
is
a
jet propeller
frass
expeller
IS
that
those frass pellets he force-fires far from his
    caterpillar fanny
smell

as good as hot-from-the-oven chocolate-chip cookies
to enemy paper wasps
and others

who would come and gobble up
that wily skipper
if he didn't make sure
that their smellers
would lead them

      someplace

         else. ❖

DiD YOU KNOW?

Frass is the name scientists use for solid food waste that comes out of the back of an insect. Some predators, like paper wasps, use the smell of frass to find their food.

Skipper butterfly caterpillars shoot their frass pellets more than three feet away from their homes. Hungry wasps are fooled into looking in the wrong place for a bite to eat.

Skippers wrap silk around leaves to make a tiny tent. Predators who want a caterpillar meal might not find the caterpillar under the leaves.

✳ How does the skipper caterpillar protect itself? Explain in your own words.

....

....

....

....

....

✳ What important ideas are hidden in the poem? Write the details that support your thoughts.

Important ideas	Details from the poem that support my thoughts

❋ Several selections in this unit relate to maintaining balance in the animal world. What are some of the most important ideas you've learned about the animal world?

....

....

....

....

....

❋ Discuss this question with a partner: how do you determine important ideas in a text? Write the three most important thoughts from your discussion.

....

....

....

....

....

....

In poems about nature, you can find important ideas that explain the natural world.

Visualizing

Think of a place you've never been but have always wanted to visit. What does it look like? What sounds would you hear? How would it feel to be there? What smells or tastes might you notice? By answering these questions, you are **visualizing.** You are using your senses to create sensory images in your mind.

You can visualize when you read, too. As you read, look for words and descriptions that appeal to your senses of sight, sound, smell, taste, and touch. The images you create in your mind will help you better understand, enjoy, and remember what you read.

The selections in this unit focus on **differences**— in people's daily life and in the natural world. As you read, you'll practice the strategy of visualizing.

Does the phrase "hot buttered popcorn" make you imagine the taste and smell of popcorn? If so, those images are called **sensory images.** A sensory image is a picture in your mind that is triggered by sensory details. A sensory detail appeals to your senses of sight, hearing, taste, smell, and touch (or how something feels). Authors often include sensory details to help you **visualize** what they write.

In this poem, María is surprised when she sees her teacher in the market. As you read, underline phrases that create strong sensory images. In the **Response Notes**, write about the images they create.

Response Notes

I can almost feel the soft, round tomatoes in my hands.

I can see Maria hiding and peeking.

My Teacher in the Market by Gary Soto

Who would suppose
On a Saturday
That my teacher
Would balance
Tomatoes in her hands
And sniff them
Right under my nose.
I'm María,
The girl with a Band-Aid
On each knee,
Pink scars the shape
Of check marks
On homework.
I'm hiding by the bags
Of potatoes,
Tiptoeing and curious.
I've never seen
My teacher in jeans
And a T-shirt,
And tennies with a hole
Where the little

Toe rubs. She
Bags the tomatoes
And a pinch of chiles.
She presses a thumb
Gently into ripe avocados,
Three for a dollar
Because they're black,
Black, but pretty black.
I wave to my teacher
And then duck,
Giggling. I look up.
She lifts a watermelon
Into her arms,
Melon with its army
Of seeds to spit
Across a sidewalk.
I can't imagine *her* doing *that*,
My teacher, my teacher.
She weighs nectarines
And plums, peaches
With their belly
Of itchy fur.
I wave again,
And duck. It's funny
Seeing my teacher
Drop a grape
Into her mouth,
Same mouth that says
4 times 6 is 36,
I mean 24. She lowers
The bunch of grapes
Into a plastic bag.
Then she turns
Toward the potatoes
And finds me peeking through.
When she says,
"Oh, it's María,
My little potato eyes,"

I blush and squint my eyes shut.
When I open them,
She's gone,
Her shopping cart
Now swinging
Down the aisle
Of cereals,
Leaving me,
María, little potato eyes. ❖

✳ Look back at the phrases you underlined. Write the three phrases that created the strongest images for you. Describe the images.

Phrase	Description of image it creates

✳ Choose one of the phrases from the chart on page 96.
Draw a picture of the image you see.

✳ Write about a time when you were surprised. What
happened? Why were you surprised? When you
are finished writing, ask a partner to read
what you wrote. Have your partner underline
phrases that create mental images for him
or her.

Look for sensory
details to help you create
strong images.

A conversation between characters is called a **dialogue**. Dialogues often spark strong sensory images.

In this chapter from the novel *How to Eat Fried Worms*, the characters are talking about eating foods they don't like. Notice the sensory details that create strong mental images. As you read, underline text that creates strong mental images. In the **Response Notes**, draw or write about the images.

Response Notes

from How to Eat Fried Worms
by Thomas Rockwell

"Hey, *Tom!* Where were you last night?"

"Yeah, you missed it."

Alan and Billy came up the front walk. Tom was sitting on his porch steps, bouncing a tennis ball.

"Old Man Tator caught Joe as we were climbing through the fence, so we all had to go back, and he made us pile the peaches on his kitchen table, and then he called our mothers."

"Joe's mother hasn't let him out yet."

"Where were you?"

Tom stopped bouncing the tennis ball. He was a tall, skinny boy who took his troubles very seriously.

"My mother kept me in."

"What for?"

"I wouldn't eat my dinner."

Alan sat down on the step below Tom and began to chew his thumbnail.

"What was it?"

"Salmon casserole."

Billy flopped down on the grass, chunky, snubnosed, freckled.

"Salmon casserole's not so bad."

"Wouldn't she let you just eat two bites?" asked Alan. "Sometimes my mother says, well, all right, if I'll just eat two bites."

"I wouldn't eat even one."

"That's stupid," said Billy. "One bite can't hurt you. I'd eat one bite of anything before I'd let them send me up to my room right after supper."

Tom shrugged.

"How about mud?" Alan asked Billy. "You wouldn't eat a bite of mud."

Alan argued a lot, small, knobby-kneed, nervous, gnawing at his thumbnail, his face smudged, his red hair mussed, shirttail hanging out, shoelaces untied.

"Sure, I would," Billy said. "Mud. What's mud? Just dirt with a little water in it. My father says everyone eats a pound of dirt every year anyway."

"How about poison?"

"That's different." Billy rolled over on his back.

"Is your mother going to make you eat the leftovers today at lunch?" he asked Tom.

"She never has before."

"How about worms?" Alan asked Billy.

Tom's sister's cat squirmed out from under the porch and rubbed against Billy's knee.

"Sure," said Billy. "Why not? Worms are just dirt."

"Yeah, but they bleed."

"So you'd have to cook them. Cows bleed."

"I bet a hundred dollars you wouldn't really eat a worm. You talk big now, but you wouldn't if you were sitting at the dinner table with a worm on your plate."

"I bet I would. I'd eat *fifteen* worms if somebody'd bet me a hundred dollars."

"You really want to bet? *I'll* bet you fifty dollars you can't eat fifteen worms. I really will."

"Where're you going to get fifty dollars?"

"In my savings account. I've got one hundred and thirty dollars and seventy-nine cents in my savings account. I know, because last week I put in the five dollars my grandmother gave me for my birthday."

"Your mother wouldn't let you take it out."

"She would if I lost the bet. She'd have to. I'd tell her I was going to sell my stamp collection otherwise. And I bought that with all my own money that I earned mowing lawns, so I can do whatever I want with it. I'll bet you fifty dollars you can't eat fifteen worms. Come on. You're chicken. You know you can't do it."

"*I* wouldn't do it," said Tom. "If salmon casserole makes me sick, think what fifteen worms would do."

Joe came scuffing up the walk and flopped down beside Billy. He was a small boy, with dark hair and a long nose and big brown eyes.

"What's going on?"

"Come on," said Alan to Billy. "Tom can be your second and Joe'll be mine, just like in a duel. You think it's so easy—here's your chance to make fifty bucks."

Billy dangled a leaf in front of the cat, but the cat just rubbed against his knee, purring.

"What kind of worms?"

"Regular worms."

"Not those big green ones that get on the tomatoes. I won't eat those. And I won't eat them all at once. It might make me sick. One worm a day for fifteen days."

"And he can eat them any way he wants," said Tom. "Boiled, stewed, fried, fricasseed."

"Yeah, but we provide the worms," said Joe.

"And there have to be witnesses present when he eats them; either me or Alan or somebody we can trust. Not just you and Billy."

"Okay?" Alan said to Billy.

Billy scratched the cat's ears. Fifty dollars. That was a lot of money. How bad could a worm taste? He'd eaten fried liver, salmon loaf, mushrooms, tongue, pig's feet. Other kids' parents were always nagging them to eat, eat; his had begun to worry about *how much* he ate. Not that he was *fat*. He just hadn't worked off all his winter blubber yet.

He slid his hand into his shirt and furtively squeezed the side of his stomach. Worms were just dirt; dirt wasn't fattening.

If he won fifty dollars, he could buy that mini-bike George Cunningham's brother had promised to sell him in September before he went away to college. Heck, he could gag *anything* down for fifty dollars, couldn't he?

He looked up. "I can use ketchup or mustard or anything like that? As much as I want?"

Alan nodded. "Okay?"

Billy stood up.

"Okay." ❖

✳ **What is one of the strongest sensory images from the selection? Write about it.**

✳ **What do Billy's words and actions tell you about him?**

....

....

....

....

....

....

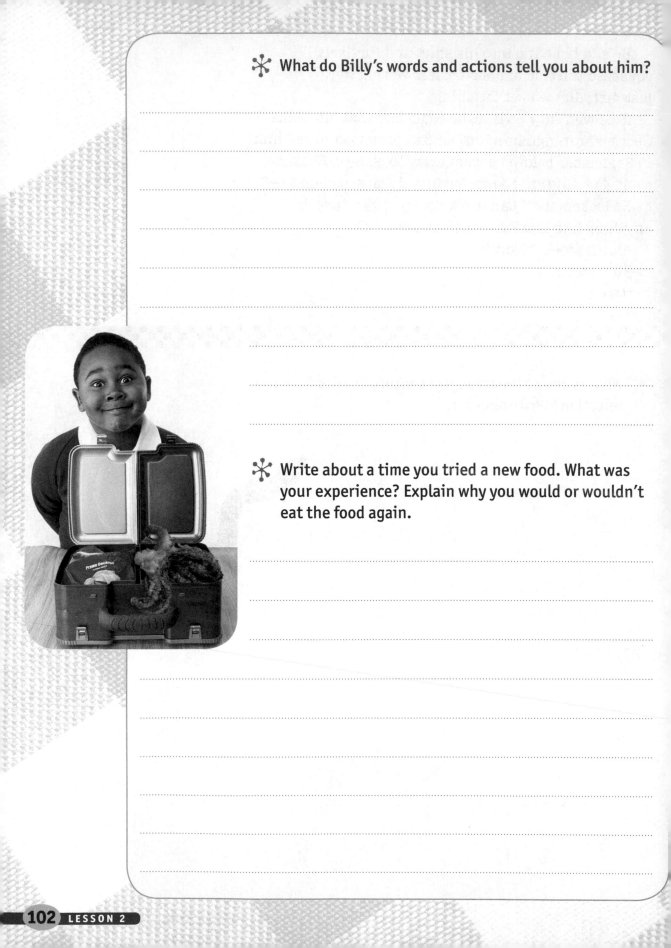

✳ **Write about a time you tried a new food. What was your experience? Explain why you would or wouldn't eat the food again.**

....

....

....

....

....

....

....

....

✳ Write a dialogue between two people who are talking about eating an unusual food. Remember to show quotation marks around the spoken words. When you finish, ask a partner to underline phrases that create strong mental images.

Look for strong images in characters' conversations.

You can learn a lot about a character by how he or she reacts to a situation. Studying **a character's reactions** will help you create a strong mental image of him or her.

In this excerpt from the novel *Double Fudge*, Fudge, Mom, Pete, and Tootsie go to a shoe store. Notice the characters' reactions to events and to each other.

As you read, underline characters' reactions that create strong mental images. In the **Response Notes**, sketch or write about the images.

from Double Fudge by Judy Blume

A couple of days before school started we went to Harry's, the shoe store on Broadway. When he was three, Fudge only wanted to wear the same shoes as me. Now he has his own ideas. But this time he couldn't decide between black with silver trim or white with blue; between lace-ups, Velcro closings, or pull-ons; between hi-tops or low. "I'll just get two pairs," he told Mom. "Maybe three." He licked his yellow lollipop, which he'd begged for before the salesman had even measured his feet.

"You need one pair of shoes and one pair of winter boots," Mom said, checking her list, "and unless you get going we won't have time to get your winter boots today."

There were at least a dozen open shoeboxes in front of Fudge, and the salesman—his name badge said *Mitch McCall*—kept checking his watch, like he was already late for some important appointment. Tootsie sat in her stroller kicking her feet, or maybe she was admiring her new shoes. Finally, I said to Fudge, "Why don't you just get the same shoes as me?"

"No thanks, Pete," Fudge said. "Your new shoes aren't that cool."

"What do you mean?" I asked, looking down at my feet.

"I mean *cool*, Pete."

"What's not cool about them?"

"Nothing's cool about them."

Could he be right? I wondered. *Did I choose too fast just to be done with it? I do that sometimes. I can't help myself. I hate to shop. But are these shoes really that bad? Bad enough so the kids at school will laugh and say, "Nice shoes, Hatcher. Where'd you find them . . . in the trash?" Should I try on another pair? Should I wait to see what Fudge chooses and then . . . Wait a minute,* I told myself. *I can't believe I'm thinking this way, as if my five-year-old brother knows more about cool than me. Since when is he the expert on cool? Since when is he the expert on anything?*

"Make up your mind," Mom told Fudge.

"I can't," Fudge said. He was wearing one style on his right foot and another on his left. "I have to have them both."

"I'll count to twenty," Mom said, "while you decide."

"I'm not deciding," Fudge told her.

"You want me to decide for you?" Mom asked.

"No!"

Tootsie mimicked him. "No!" Then she grabbed the yellow lollipop out of Fudge's hand and threw it. It hit Mitch McCall in the head, stuck to his hair, and hung there like an ornament on a Christmas tree.

"Tootsie!" Mom cried. "That wasn't polite." But Tootsie laughed and clapped her sticky little hands anyway.

Mitch McCall grimaced as he pulled the lollipop off his head. It took some hairs with it, which really seemed to upset him, probably because he was already kind of bald on top.

"I'm so sorry," Mom said, handing him a Wetwipe from her bag.

"Maybe you would prefer another salesperson," Mitch McCall said, through teeth so tightly clenched his mouth hardly opened at all.

"No," Mom said, "you've been very helpful."

"All right then," Mitch McCall said, kneeling in front of Fudge. "Let's get this over with. Make up your mind, son. There are other customers waiting." ❖

 Fudge tells Pete that Pete's shoes are not cool. Look back at Pete's reaction. What does Pete's reaction tell you about his personality?

 Think about the reactions that Pete has to his little brother. What connections can you make with his experiences?

✳ Make a comic strip that shows what happened at the shoe store. Create speech bubbles for the characters.

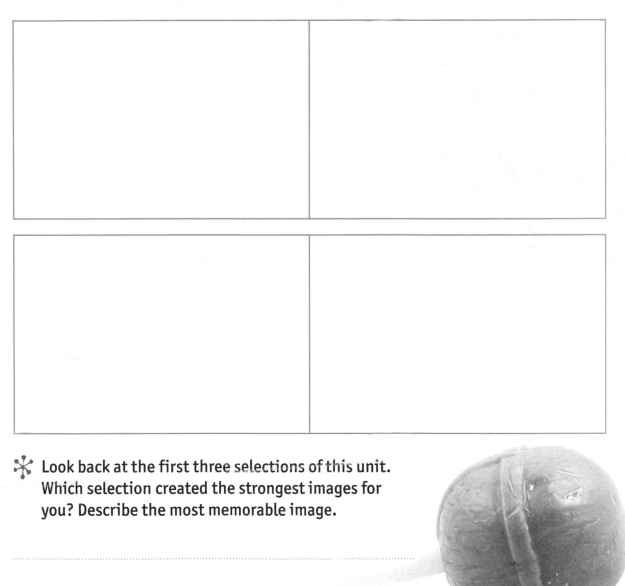

✳ Look back at the first three selections of this unit. Which selection created the strongest images for you? Describe the most memorable image.

....

....

....

....

....

....

Study characters' reactions to create strong mental images.

Each person has a **point of view**, or a way of looking at things. You can create strong mental images from a person's or character's point of view. In this excerpt from the nonfiction book *Quilted Landscape,* Carlos Nuñez speaks in the first person and tells about his life. His point of view will help you create images of his life and your own.

As you read, underline text that shows Carlos's point of view. In the **Response Notes**, write what you learn about Carlos.

Response Notes

Carlos Nuñez from *Quilted Landscape*
by Yale Strom

I liked school in Santo Domingo because I had a lot of friends. We would play lots of different games. My favorites were Monopoly, basketball and baseball.

I came to America in 1993. My grandfather came to Dominican to get my mother, aunt, cousin, and myself. This was the first time I had ever been on an airplane.

Over there you only hear Spanish being spoken, never English. Here in my neighborhood you hear Spanish and English. We lived in a house, which I like better than the apartment we have here. There I played with my cousins downstairs outside. Here my mother won't let me play outside. I have to play in the house. She thinks something's going to happen to me. There is trouble sometimes, even killings happening in our neighborhood. My mother is afraid that I could be hurt.

I'll never forget how to speak Spanish. If I forget I won't be able to speak to my mother. Then I won't be able to tell what I want her to buy and where and when I want to go somewhere.

Coming here wasn't difficult for me because I like traveling to new places. What I think about most is I will never be able to save enough money to be able to visit my homeland, my friends and cousins.

My mother read something to me from the newspaper about people in America who don't like new immigrants. This makes me sad. These people come here to get a better life, to get a better education. My mother came here to get a better life. And these people who speak badly about new immigrants forget that their people once came from another country too. Maybe many years ago these people should not have been allowed to come and stay here.

I live with my mother, sister, cousin, my other cousin, my aunt and my other aunt and my grandpa all in two rooms. I sleep in a bed with my mother and sister. My two aunts and two cousins sleep in another bed and my grandpa, he sleeps in the hallway on a sofa between the bedroom and the toilet.

We have to stay here for now because my mother doesn't have enough money to get another house. She is working to get another house.

My father lives in Dominican. I don't know if he will move here or not. My mother takes me to this store where you can call people who live far away and I speak with my father. I miss him because he would take me places, like the beach and park and we would play baseball. My sister or mother don't play baseball with me.

I play trombone and French horn after school in Mr. Mac's class. We play the song "Rose con Leche." I don't practice at home because my mother doesn't want to hear me blowing in such a small house, and she says the instrument

could get lost. When I am older I will become a music teacher like Mr. Mac. I like playing and teaching other kids how to play music. At home I listen to Spanish, reggae, and rap music, but Spanish is my favorite kind.

I like going to a school like PS 20 that has students from different countries. I learn about their customs, food, and games. In this school I have met students from Bangladesh, Japan, China, Mexico, and Peru. But I guess if you think about it one day New York could fill up with too many people. It seems everyone from other countries wants to come here and live. When it becomes too crowded here then those moving here might go instead to Nebraska or Montana. I'm sure the streets are cleaner there than they are in New York City. ❖

✳ How do you think Carlos feels about living in New York City? Why do you think he feels that way?

✳ In the space below, draw an image of New York City that you created from reading about Carlos and his experiences. Write a detailed caption about your drawing.

✳ Choose two or three details that are important to understanding Carlos. Why are they important?

Looking at events through a character's eyes can help you create strong images.

Authors often use details that appeal to the **five senses**—sight, smell, hearing, taste, and touch. These details help you create strong mental images.

The passage below is from the nonfiction book *Bodies from the Ash*. It tells about the eruption of Mt. Vesuvius, a volcano in Italy. This eruption happened in ancient times.

As you read, underline details that appeal to your senses. In the **Response Notes**, list the senses you use.

Response Notes

Bodies from the Ash by James M. Deem

People in Pompeii might have noticed the small cloud that morning and may have felt tremors, but they continued with their daily activities until early that afternoon. At one o'clock, eighty-one loaves of bread were baking in the ovens of the Modestus bakery, and vendors were selling fruit and other products in the *macellum*, or marketplace. The priests in the Temple of Isis were preparing to eat an afternoon meal of eggs and fish. It was then that Vesuvius finally awoke with a massive explosion.

An enormous pine-tree-shaped cloud of ash, pumice, and larger rock fragments blasted into the air. Within a half-hour, the cloud had risen over ten miles high, and winds had blown it toward the southeast—in the direction of Pompeii. The cloud blocked the sun and turned the sky over Pompeii to night. Then it began to release a deluge of ash, lightweight white pumice stones, and some larger, heavier volcanic rocks on Pompeii. At the same time, earth tremors continued to shake the town.

At first, most people would have taken shelter in their homes or other buildings. But as the volcanic fallout began to accumulate at the rate of five or six inches per hour and the pumice grew to an inch in size, many decided to escape. Protecting themselves as best as they could from the falling stones, they headed down the narrow city streets, stepping on the accumulated fallout, toward one of the city gates. Some people used pillows and blankets tied to their heads; others shielded themselves with pans or even baskets. After reaching the gates, many took the coast road; others tried to escape by sea. But the buoyant pumice floated in the water, filling the harbor and making a seagoing escape more difficult. During this time, some were killed on their way out of the city, hit by larger rocks falling from the eruption cloud.

By five-thirty that afternoon, two feet of ash and stones had accumulated in the streets, on roofs, and in open areas such as the courtyards of houses and gardens. In fact, so much pumice had built up on roofs that some buildings began to collapse, especially when the loose pumice was shaken by strong earth tremors. Many Pompeians were crushed in their houses when the roofs caved in on them.

As the evening progressed, the raining pumice turned from white to gray and grew bigger, some pieces almost three inches in size. By midnight, first-story doors and windows were completely blocked by fallout. Anyone who had delayed escape would have had to use a second-floor window to reach the street and then walk atop five feet or more of collected stones and ash. Fires were burning on the slopes of Vesuvius. Lightning filled the sky around it, and the eruption cloud had risen almost twenty miles high. But no one in Pompeii would have been able to see this. ❖

✳ Choose three events from the selection. Write them below. Then write the senses they triggered. One has been done for you.

Events from the selection	Senses they triggered
"An enormous pine-tree-shaped cloud of ash, pumice, and larger rock fragments blasted into the air."	sight and hearing

✳ What questions do you have about the selection?
Write two of them below. Then discuss your questions
with a partner. Were you able to figure out any
answers? Write notes about the answers you found.

....

....

....

....

....

✳ How do you think people would be warned of a
volcano eruption today? What tools are used now
that hadn't been invented during the time of the
Mt. Vesuvius eruption?

....

....

....

....

....

....

As you read, look for
details that appeal to a
variety of senses.

You make decisions everyday. Some decisions are small, and some are large. Some decisions can make a big difference in your life and in the lives of others. Thinking about **the decisions of characters** or people can create strong mental images.

In this excerpt from the nonfiction book *Blizzard!* you'll read about an important decision one teacher made. The blizzard happened in March 1888.

As you read, underline the decisions the teacher made. Write about the decisions in the **Response Notes**.

Response Notes

from **Blizzard!** by Jim Murphy

A young teacher in southern Vermont wasn't surprised in the least to begin classes that morning with every seat occupied. Deep snow was fairly common in the area and the local people weren't about to let a little bad weather stand in the way of their children's education. So this teacher taught lessons through the morning and into the early afternoon.

He grew worried when the storm increased in ferocity at noon, and then alarmed when he saw that a snowdrift was almost up to the windowsill on one side of the building. He decided to dismiss classes early, though he hesitated to send his pupils out on their own. Some of the children were so young and small that the snow on the ground was already over their heads.

His solution to the problem was as straightforward and practical as the people in the area were: He tied a rope to all fourteen of his students, with him and several of the larger students in front to break a trail. Then he led them out into the storm, going from one child's home to the next until each had been delivered safely. His school day finally over, he went home to milk and feed his cows. It would be three weeks before the roads were clear enough to resume classes.

This schoolmaster and his charges were fortunate. They were young and healthy, so their bodies could withstand the battering of the storm. ❖

✳ Think about the main decision the teacher made. Draw three pictures to show what happened as a result of the decision.

✳ Make a connection with a time when you experienced extreme weather. Describe what happened.

Imagine that you have to explain visualizing to a new classmate. Write your explanation below. Tell how visualizing helped you understand one of the selections in this unit.

....

....

....

....

....

....

 Choose one character or person from a selection in this unit. Compare yourself with him or her. How are you alike? How are you different?

....

....

....

....

....

....

A character's decision can create a strong mental image.

Making Inferences

You and a friend are watching TV at your house. A scratching sound comes from inside the closet. Your friend looks scared. You look around to see if your kitten is nearby. She's not. You say, "Don't worry. That must be my kitten." You open the door and out she runs.

You have just **made an inference**. You combined clues that you noticed with what you already know. The clues were the noise and the missing kitten. You inferred that your kitten was locked in the closet and was scratching to get out.

You can make inferences when you read, too. An inference can be a prediction, a conclusion, or an interpretation.

In this unit, you'll read about different kinds of **relationships**. You will practice making inferences to better understand your reading.

INFERENCES AND ACTIONS

You can learn a lot about a character by studying his or her actions. You can learn even more about a character by **making inferences** about his or her actions. Here's how to make an inference about a character:

- Find a detail about something a character does.
- Think about what that detail tells you about the character.
- Your new thought about the character is your inference.

The selection below is called "Teeth." It's from a memoir by Ralph Fletcher. A **memoir** is a true piece of writing similar to an autobiography. As you read, underline some of the actions of Great Grandma and the narrator. In the **Response Notes**, write what you infer about each character on the basis of his or her actions.

Response Notes

Teeth by Ralph Fletcher

Mom had a "tooth bank" shaped like a coconut. When one of our teeth came out, she washed off the blood and deposited the tooth into that bank.

"Why are you saving our teeth?" Jimmy wanted to know.

"Because." She smiled at him. "They're precious to me. And so are you."

Great Grandma came to visit two or three times a year. She was old and tiny. Great Grandma always wore a gray sweatshirt way too big for her and smelled like the gingersnap cookies she baked. <u>She put whole chunks of ginger into the cookies, so when I bit into them, they made my eyes water.</u> I loved her with all my heart and pretended to love those cookies so I wouldn't hurt her feelings.

Great Grandma had a slow walk, and I liked to secretly follow her as she moved through the house or out in the yard. Her hearing wasn't very good so she never knew when I was spying on her.

Great Grandma probably didn't know he didn't like the ginger chunks.

Early one morning I heard her outside my bedroom, going downstairs. I waited until she reached the bottom stair before I got out of bed and followed her. She padded into the kitchen, dressed in slippers and the gray sweatshirt. What was she doing? Getting a snack? Making coffee? Moving closer, careful to stay out of sight, I saw her go into the pantry. I was amazed when she came out holding the tooth bank! She unscrewed the rubber plug on the bottom, emptied some teeth into her hand, and went out the back door.

❋ What do you predict Great Grandma will do with the teeth?

....

....

....

I knew if I followed too closely she'd catch me spying, so I eased out the front door and ran around the house. The grass was a cold, wet shock to my bare feet. Stealing from tree to tree, I saw Great Grandma go into the garage. A minute later she came out carrying a trowel, then went to the vegetable garden in back of the house.

I crept up until I was about thirty feet away, close enough to see her kneel down and start digging a hole in the ground. She put one of the teeth into the hole, covered it with dirt, and patted it down. She did the same thing three more times. Then she turned around and moved slowly back toward the house.

I made myself wait five minutes, then five more, before going to the garden spot where she planted our teeth. I don't know what I expected to see. Finally, I went inside and snuck up to my bedroom.

I never told anyone about this, and Great Grandma never said anything, but I had a million questions in my head. Did she plant the teeth figuring they'd bring good luck to our house? Did she think they'd fertilize the tomatoes? Was she just plain crazy?

I never figured out what she was doing that morning. Nothing unusual sprouted in the garden that summer. But every time I went past that spot, I'd check to see if one of those teeth had taken root in the soil and started to grow. ❖

✳ Think about the actions of Great Grandma and the narrator. List a few actions you noticed for each character and write the inferences you can make.

Narrator's action	Inference about the narrator
He secretly followed Great Grandma.	He didn't want Great Grandma to know that he was spying on her.

Great Grandma's action	Inference about Great Grandma

* Why do you think Great Grandma buried the teeth?

....

....

....

....

* What happens in your family when a child loses a tooth? Ask a partner the same question. Write about how your tooth traditions are similar and different.

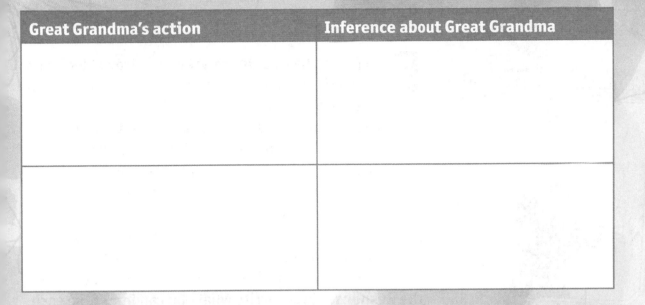

....

....

....

....

....

Thinking about a character's actions will help you make inferences about him or her.

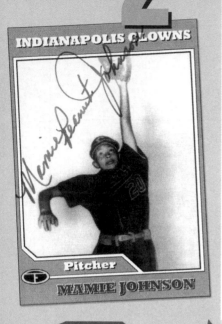

INDIANAPOLIS CLOWNS

Pitcher

MAMIE JOHNSON

Each person has a **point of view**, or a way of looking at something. Your point of view about an event may be different from someone else's.

Sometimes authors show the same event through two points of view. You can use the points of view to make inferences about the characters and the event. Making inferences will help you better understand the text.

Mamie Johnson was one of only three women who played professional baseball in the Negro Leagues. As you read from her **biography**, underline text that shows both Mamie's point of view and Mama's point of view. In the **Response Notes**, write what you can infer from each person's point of view. Remember, an inference is a prediction, a conclusion, or an interpretation.

from A Strong Right Arm by Michelle Y. Green

Sleeping that night was like trying to get butter from a duck. It was downright impossible. I kept turning things over in my mind: everything I had learned, everywhere I had been, and how everything I'd hoped for was resting on this day. I remembered my days at Grandma's house, where it all started, and my nights of talking to those big old stars. In Washington, D.C., streetlights hid the stars most nights. And tonight, on this important night, cloud cover kept even the few I was usually able to find hidden from sight. I strained to see just one from my bedroom window in Mama's house. Even the stars were telling me: "You're on your own this time."

When Mama came to wake me at 7:00 in the morning, my head was still resting on the windowsill where I had fallen asleep.

"Come on, baby," she said. "Get yourself washed up while I make you a good breakfast."

In no time, I was sitting at Mama's table staring into a plate of eggs, grits, and toast.

"Try and eat a little something, Mamie. You need your strength."

I stabbed at the yolk of my fried egg in silence.

"You know I want to be there with you today, honey," she said, grabbing me firm around both shoulders. "But it's not easy changing shifts on short notice."

"I know, Mama." I smiled up at her. It was rare Mama ever missed a day's work as a dietician at Freedman's Hospital. I think it was because she liked helping people so much and she knew they depended on her. And raising a daughter on her own, she couldn't afford to lose a single day's pay.

"Why don't you stop messing with that plate, and go ahead and get out of here," she fussed.

"I'm sorry, Mama. I guess these butterflies flitting around my insides don't leave much room for grits."

"Child, I don't know what you're so nervous about," she said. "I've watched you grow up, both up close and at a distance. I've never known you to be afraid of anything." She turned me around by the shoulders and looked me straight in the eye.

"You go on out there and do like you always do, Mamie. You give it your best."

"I will, Mama," I said, my throat as dry as the cold toast on my plate.

"How many times have you told me that this is what you were born to do?" she continued. "Now, if that's true, all you gotta do is go out there and be yourself. And if they don't like what they see, then they're the losers, not you."

"Thanks, Mama," I said, squeezing both her hands hard like that day at Grandma's creek.

"You'll be just fine, honey," she said, turning to leave. "Besides, I prayed you up real good last night. You got exact change for the streetcar?"

"Yes, Mama, I got everything I need."

"You sure do, honey," she said, blowing me a kiss from the door.

Getting there at 9:30 for a 10:00 date, I thought I'd be early. But when I got to the field, I was surprised to see a bunch of folks already there. What I didn't see was anybody else that didn't know anyone but me. I was the only one trying out! ❖

✳ Look back at the passage where Mamie says, "Even the stars were telling me: 'You're on your own this time.'" What inferences can you make about how Mamie is feeling?

✳ What can you infer about Mamie's and Mama's relationship?

✳ In the Venn diagram below, list details about Mamie's and Mama's points of view about the tryouts. How are their points of view similar? How are they different?

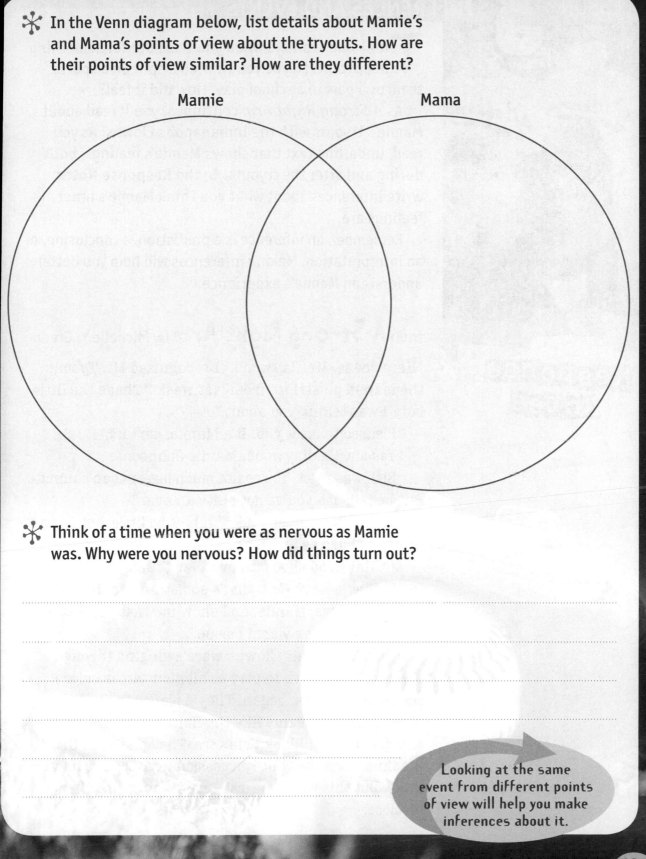

Mamie   Mama

✳ Think of a time when you were as nervous as Mamie was. Why were you nervous? How did things turn out?

....

....

....

....

....

Looking at the same event from different points of view will help you make inferences about it.

Think about a time when you tried out for something important. Maybe you wanted a spot on a sports team or a part in a school play. How did it feel?

As *A Strong Right Arm* continues, you'll read about Mamie's tryouts with the Indianapolis Clowns. As you read, underline text that shows Mamie's feelings, both during and after the tryouts. In the **Response Notes**, write inferences about what you think Mamie's inner feelings are.

Remember, an inference is a prediction, a conclusion, or an interpretation. Making inferences will help you better understand Mamie's experience.

Response Notes

from **A Strong Right Arm** by Michelle Y. Green

"Here she is, Mr. Haywood." I recognized Mr. Tyson, the man in pinstripes from last week. "That's the little lady I was telling you about."

"Pleased to meet you. It's Mamie, isn't it?"

"Yes sir, Mr. Haywood. Mamie Johnson."

"Bish was right. You're not much bigger than a minute. But he tells me you've got quite an arm."

"Thank you, sir," I said. "I might be little, but I can throw as hard as any man."

Mr. Haywood shook all over, laughing.

"Is that a fact? Well, that's something I'd like to see. Go on out there, Mamie, and show us what you got. All right, you all, let's warm her up."

The Indianapolis Clowns were swinging through town for a few days to play exhibition games before the regular season began. They'd played in Washington before, meeting teams like the Baltimore Black Barons and Washington Black Senators. They played in Griffith Stadium when the white professional baseball team was away. But this was the first time I was seeing them up close.

For the next hour, I played side by side with real ballplayers—Ted Richardson, Gordon "Hoppy" Hopkins, Junior Hamilton, and to my surprise, another lady baseball player, Lyle "Toni" Stone. They had me pitching to some of the best hitters in the league, asking me to try the pitches I knew and the ones I didn't. Then fielding. I was partial to shortstop, because it was closest to the mound, but they kept me rotating to see where I could fit in best. What surprised them as much as my pitching was my ability to hit. Sure, I did my share of swatting the breeze—I'd never been up against the likes of these fellas before. But I got my share of good cuts too—enough to let them know I could hold my own in the batter's box.

I can't remember exactly when I stopped being nervous, because I was having so much fun. When it was all over, Mr. Haywood seemed like he couldn't stop grinning. He shook my hand till it felt like it was gonna clean fall off, and then he took me to meet the team's business manager, McKinley Downs.

"Call me Bunny," he said, pumping my hand some more.

"Bunny," said Mr. Haywood, "you know what to do."

Seventeen years of waiting, and the only thing now between me and my dream was my name in ink on the bottom of the paper Bunny Downs was putting in my hands. I tell you, he didn't have to twist my arm one bit. This was the same Bunny Downs who just last year picked up some new cross-handed hitter from the sandlots down south. That slugger had been signed by the Milwaukee Braves after only two months. His name was Hank Aaron.

They say God made the world in one week. But I don't think that was his biggest miracle. It had taken me all of my seventeen years to make it to this point. It only took the Good Lord seven days to take me all the way from the sandlots to a front seat on the Indianapolis Clowns' team bus. Me and my new teammates were heading down south to spring training. ❖

✳ In the chart below, write inferences you can make from each of the events.

Event	Inference
The Indianapolis Clowns watch Mamie play at different positions.	
Mamie plays next to the pros for an hour.	
Mamie signs a contract.	

✳ Write a diary entry that Mamie might have written the evening after her tryout.

Dear Diary,

✳ Choose one of the selections you have read so far in this unit. Explain how making inferences made your reading meaningful.

....

....

....

....

....

....

Making inferences about characters and events deepens your understanding of a character's feelings.

When you learn new information about a topic, you can make inferences and create new understandings.

For hundreds of years, people have believed that a monster lives in the Scottish lake Loch Ness. Photographs seem to show the monster. Many people have stories about it. Scientists have been studying the lake for a long time.

As you read this nonfiction piece about the Loch Ness monster, underline new facts you learn. In the **Response Notes**, write inferences or new understandings that the facts create for you.

Response Notes

The Loch Ness Monster by Milly Vranes

Loch Ness is one of the largest lakes in Scotland. The first record of a monster in the lake was written down in 565. In Saint Columbia's autobiography, he tells of a swimmer who was killed by a hungry lake monster. Although there were many ancient legends about monsters, this account made the Loch Ness monster famous.

When a new road was built along the edge of the lake in 1933, the number of sightings of the monster soared. In 1934, a young veterinary student was riding a motorcycle. He claimed that he nearly ran into the monster as it crossed the road.

Most sightings made by people seem to agree that the monster looks like a plesiosaur. Plesiosaurs were aquatic reptiles that lived from the Triassic period to the Jurassic period. This was about 230–144 million years ago. The plesiosaur had a roundish, bulky body and tapering tail. It had a long neck and a small head. It also had two flippers that helped to propel it through the water.

Probably one of the first photographs of the monster was taken in 1933 by a man named Hugh Gray. He said that he did not see any head, but that there was a lot of movement in the water.

The "surgeon's photograph" is probably the most famous picture of the monster. In 1993, though, a man named Christian Spurling admitted that the photograph was a fake. He had helped build the model monster that was photographed.

On a clear day in August 1996, Austin Hepburn saw movement in the waters of Loch Ness. The photographs he took show a wake. There was no wind that day. No boats were in the area.

Many scientists have tried to find out whether the monster really exists. Sonar and other high-tech equipment have been used. Research is still being carried out to this day. But the water of the lake is dark and murky. This makes it difficult to take any clear pictures. No conclusive evidence has ever been found to prove or disprove the legend.

However, one investigation helped to fuel the mystery. Something very large was detected under the water, but scientists still cannot agree on what their equipment detected.

Can it be possible that a prehistoric creature still exists beneath the deep and murky waters of Loch Ness? ❖

Computer-generated image of a plesiosaur

✳ What are two new facts you learned from the selection?

....

....

....

....

....

✳ In the chart, write an inference you can make from each key piece of information.

Key information	Inference
The "surgeon's photograph" was a fake.	The surgeon wanted people to believe he really saw the monster.
The water of the lake is dark and murky.	
In August 1996 there was movement in the Loch Ness waters on a windless day.	

✳ Do you think the Loch Ness monster exists? Write a paragraph stating your opinion. To help you plan your paragraph, fill in the chart first. Write your reasons and then list details from the selection that support each one.

Reason I think the Loch Ness monster exists OR doesn't exist	Details from the selection that support the reason

Now write your paragraph.

....

....

....

....

....

....

Learning new information will help you make inferences and create new understandings about a topic.

INFERENCES, IMAGES, AND EMOTIONS

Poets often use **strong images** in their poems. An image can evoke thoughts, feelings, or pictures in your mind. When you read a poem, you can make inferences based on the poem's images. An inference is a prediction, a conclusion, or an interpretation.

The poem you'll read tells about a relationship formed during a war. As you read, underline strong images. In the **Response Notes**, write your feelings and any inferences you make about the images.

Response Notes

The Friend I Met While Running from the War by Song Myong-ho

He went away
his father carrying him piggyback,
following the brook
where the clouds rush noisily by,
the friend I met while running from the
   war.

When the cannons' roar
came over the mountain ridge,
the cicadas stopped singing
and there was only the barking of the
   dog
keeping watch alone
in the house of camellias
behind the garden walls.

We would take turns eating
mouthfuls of wild strawberries
and share green apples,
the friend whose name I never knew,
running from the war.

In June,
my friend's face
rises
in the clouds of flowers.

Dearer than a hometown friend,
I haven't heard from him since,
the friend I met while running from the
    war. ❖

❊ In the chart, describe two strong images from the
poem. List the senses each image evokes. Then write
an inference you can make about the image.

Image	Senses or feelings it evokes	My inference about the image

Images in poems
can spark emotions and
help you make inferences

You can learn a lot about characters from their **interactions**, even when one of the characters is a dog. Studying the interactions and making inferences from them will deepen your understanding of the characters and plot.

In this excerpt from the novel *Because of Winn-Dixie*, Opal finds a stray dog at the grocery store. As you read, underline parts of the text that show interactions. In the **Response Notes**, write inferences about the interactions.

Response Notes

from **Because of Winn-Dixie**
by Kate DiCamillo

That summer I found Winn-Dixie was also the summer me and the preacher moved to Naomi, Florida, so he could be the new preacher at the Open Arms Baptist Church of Naomi. My daddy is a good preacher and a nice man, but sometimes it's hard for me to think about him as my daddy, because he spends so much time preaching or thinking about preaching or getting ready to preach. And so, in my mind, I think of him as "the preacher." Before I was born, he was a missionary in India and that is how I got my first name. But he calls me by my second name, Opal, because that was his mother's name. And he loved her a lot.

Anyway, while me and Winn-Dixie walked home, I told him how I got my name and I told him how I had just moved to Naomi. I also told him about the preacher and how he was a good man, even if he was too distracted with sermons and prayers and suffering people to go grocery shopping.

"But you know what?" I told Winn-Dixie. "You are a suffering dog, so maybe he will take to you right away. Maybe he'll let me keep you."

Winn-Dixie looked up at me and wagged his tail. He was kind of limping like something was wrong with one of his legs. And I have to admit, he stunk. Bad. He was an ugly dog, but already, I loved him with all my heart.

When we got to the Friendly Corners Trailer Park, I told Winn-Dixie that he had to behave right and be quiet, because this was an all adult trailer park and the only reason I got to live in it was because the preacher was a preacher and I was a good, quiet kid. I was what the Friendly Corners Trailer Park manager, Mr. Alfred, called "an exception." And I told Winn-Dixie he had to act like an exception, too; specifically, I told him not to pick any fights with Mr. Alfred's cats or Mrs. Detweller's little yappie Yorkie dog, Samuel. Winn-Dixie looked up at me while I was telling him everything, and I swear he understood.

"Sit," I told him when we got to my trailer. He sat right down. He had good manners. "Stay here," I told him. "I'll be right back."

The preacher was sitting in the living room, working at the little foldout table. He had papers spread all around him and he was rubbing his nose, which always means he is thinking. Hard.

"Daddy?" I said.

"Hmmm," he said back.

"Daddy, do you know how you always tell me that we should help those less fortunate than ourselves?"

"Mmmmmm-hmmm," he said. He rubbed his nose and looked around at his papers.

"Well," I said, "I found a Less Fortunate at the grocery store."

"Is that right?" he said.

"Yes sir," I told him. I stared at the preacher really hard. Sometimes he reminded me of a turtle hiding inside its shell, in there thinking about things and not ever sticking his head out into the world. "Daddy, I was wondering. Could this Less Fortunate, could he stay with us for a while?"

Finally the preacher looked up at me. "Opal," he said, "what are you talking about?"

"I found a dog," I told him. "And I want to keep him."

"No dogs," the preacher said. "We've talked about this before. You don't need a dog."

"I know it," I said. "I know I don't need a dog. But this dog needs me. Look," I said. I went to the trailer door and I hollered, "Winn-Dixie!"

Winn-Dixie's ears shot up in the air and he grinned and sneezed, and then he came limping up the steps and into the trailer and put his head right in the preacher's lap, right on top of a pile of papers.

The preacher looked at Winn-Dixie. He looked at his ribs and his matted-up fur and the places where he was bald. The preacher's nose wrinkled up. Like I said, the dog smelled pretty bad.

Winn-Dixie looked up at the preacher. He pulled back his lips and showed the preacher all of his crooked yellow teeth and wagged his tail and knocked some of the preacher's papers off the table. Then he sneezed and some more papers fluttered to the floor.

"What did you call this dog?" the preacher asked.

"Winn-Dixie," I whispered. I was afraid to say anything too loud. I could see that Winn-Dixie was having a good effect on the preacher. He was making him poke his head out of his shell.

"Well," said the preacher. "He's a stray if I've ever seen one." He put down his pencil and scratched Winn-Dixie behind the ears. "And a Less Fortunate, too. That's for sure. Are you looking for a home?" the preacher asked, real soft, to Winn-Dixie.

Winn-Dixie wagged his tail.

"Well," the preacher said. "I guess you've found one." ❖

✳ How would you describe the interactions between the pairs of characters below? What inferences can you make from their interactions?

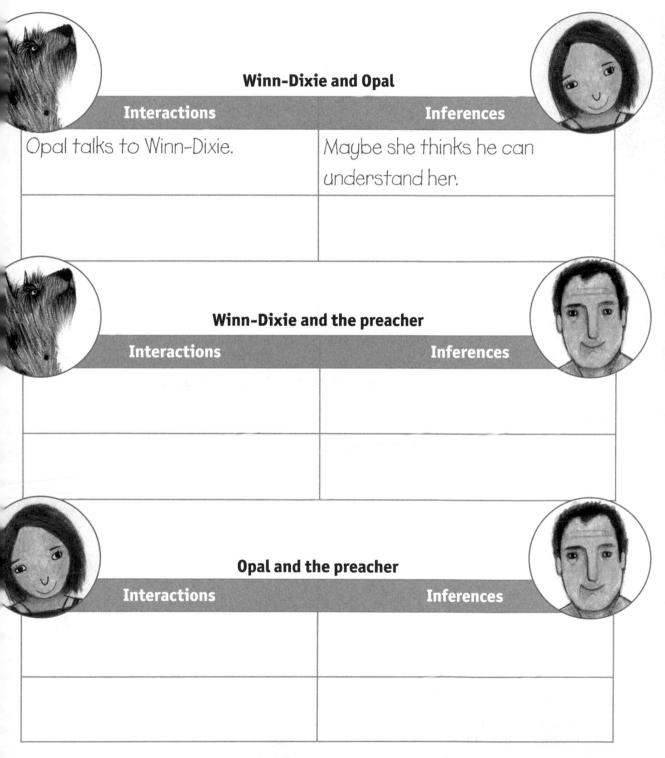

Winn-Dixie and Opal

Interactions	Inferences
Opal talks to Winn-Dixie.	Maybe she thinks he can understand her.

Winn-Dixie and the preacher

Interactions	Inferences

Opal and the preacher

Interactions	Inferences

✳ How do you connect with Opal? Have you wanted something as badly as she wants Winn-Dixie?

....
....
....
....
....
....

✳ Think about how you make inferences. Explain this process to a partner. Now write about what you understand about making inferences.

....
....
....
....
....
....
....

Thinking about interactions between characters will help you make inferences about them.

Synthesizing

Have you ever taken a long trip in the car? What do you remember about it? Did you stop for meals? Did you buy souvenirs? Did you see new places? Did you like the trip more than you thought you would? Or less?

Reading is similar to taking a trip. As you travel through a story, you stop and think, you collect new ideas, and you sometimes change your thoughts about a topic. This process of collecting new ideas and combining them with what you already know to create new ideas is called **synthesis**. During and after you read, you **synthesize** new ideas.

In this unit, you'll read about different kinds of **journeys** that people and animals take. You'll also practice synthesizing your thoughts to better understand what you read.

BIG IDEAS FROM STORY EVENTS

How do you get to know characters in a story? Sometimes an author describes the characters. Sometimes you get to know them through story events. You also learn about characters' thoughts and feelings by how they respond to the events around them. Thinking about characters' thoughts and feelings can lead you to **synthesize** big ideas about them.

In this excerpt from the novel *Maniac Magee*, you'll learn how Jeffrey responds to the events in his life.

As you read, underline sentences that tell about new story events. In the **Response Notes**, write your thoughts about each event.

Response Notes

His parents died.
He must've
felt awful.

I wonder if he'll
like his aunt
and uncle.

from Maniac Magee by Jerry Spinelli

Maniac Magee was not born in a dump. He was born in a house, a pretty ordinary house, right across the river from here, in Bridgeport. And he had regular parents, a mother and a father.

But not for long.

One day his parents left him with a sitter and took the P & W high-speed trolley into the city. On the way back home, they were on board when the P & W had its famous crash, when the motorman was drunk and took the high trestle over the Schuylkill River at sixty miles an hour, and the whole kaboodle took a swan dive into the water.

And just like that, Maniac was an orphan. He was three years old.

Of course, to be accurate, he wasn't really Maniac then. He was Jeffrey. Jeffrey Lionel Magee.

Little Jeffrey was shipped off to his nearest relatives, Aunt Dot and Uncle Dan. They lived in Hollidaysburg, in the western part of Pennsylvania.

Aunt Dot and Uncle Dan hated each other, but because they were strict Catholics, they wouldn't get a divorce. Around the time Jeffrey arrived, they stopped talking to each other. Then they stopped sharing.

Pretty soon there were two of everything in the house. Two bathrooms. Two TVs. Two refrigerators. Two toasters. If it were possible, they would have had two Jeffreys. As it was, they split him up as best they could. For instance, he would eat dinner with Aunt Dot on Monday, with Uncle Dan on Tuesday, and so on.

Eight years of that.

Then came the night of the spring musicale at Jeffrey's school. He was in the chorus. There was only one show, and one auditorium, so Aunt Dot and Uncle Dan were forced to share at least that much. Aunt Dot sat on one side, Uncle Dan on the other.

Jeffrey probably started screaming from the start of the song, which was "Talk to the Animals," but nobody knew it because he was drowned out by all the other voices. Then the music ended, and Jeffrey went right on screaming, his face bright red by now, his neck bulging. The music director faced the singers, frozen with his arms still raised. In the audience faces began to change. There was a quick smatter of giggling by some people who figured the screaming kid was some part of the show, some funny animal maybe. Then the giggling stopped, and eyes started to shift and heads started to turn, because now everybody could see that this wasn't part of the show at all, that little Jeffrey Magee wasn't supposed to be up there on the risers, pointing to his aunt and uncle, bellowing out from the midst of the chorus: "Talk! Talk, will ya! Talk! Talk! Talk!"

No one knew it then, but it was the birth scream of a legend.

And that's when the running started. Three springy steps down from the risers — girls in pastel dresses screaming, the music director lunging — a leap from the stage, out the side door and into the starry, sweet, onion-grass-smelling night.

Never again to return to the house of two toasters. Never again to return to school. ❖

✻ List three story events you underlined. What big ideas does each event tell you about Jeffrey and his experience? The big ideas are your synthesis.

Story event	What big ideas does this tell you about Jeffrey and his experience?

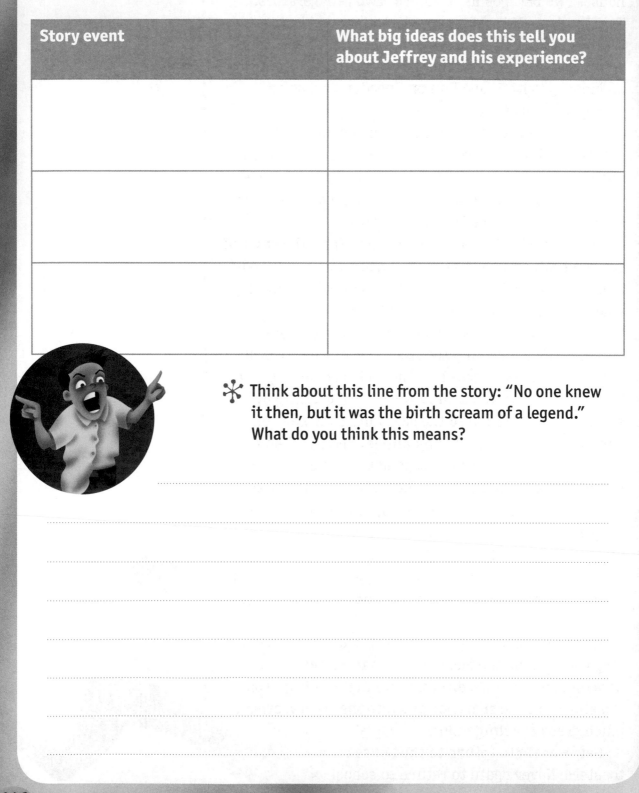

✻ Think about this line from the story: "No one knew it then, but it was the birth scream of a legend." What do you think this means?

....

....

....

....

....

....

✳ **How did your thinking about Jeffrey change as you read the selection? What made your thinking change?**

✳ **How would you describe Jeffrey's overall journey?**

As story events change, your thinking may change, too.

Change can be big or small. How characters react to change can tell you a lot about them. Studying characters' reactions to change can lead you to **synthesize** big ideas about the characters and the text.

In this excerpt from the novel *Long Journey Home*, a big change is about to happen. As you read, underline text that signals a change is about to happen. In the **Response Notes**, write your thoughts about the characters' reactions to what's going on.

from **Long Journey Home** by Julius Lester

BONG!
BONG!
BONG!

The slaves looked up at the sound of the bell. None of them could remember ever hearing the bell in the afternoon. It always woke them in the morning, and the only other time it would ring was after they came from the fields and massa wanted them to come to the big house to see someone get a whipping.

"What you reckon he called us out of the fields for, Jake?" Sarah asked the tall black man next to her.

Jake shook his head. "Don't know. You suppose what we heard about us being free is true? Maybe he's calling us to the big house to tell us we free."

Sarah laughed. "You better get that notion out of your head. If we was free, you don't think he'd ever tell us himself, do you?"

"I suppose not. Well, let's go see what it is. He probably done sold all of us and our new massa is waiting to take us."

"That's more like the truth."

As Jake and Sarah started to leave the field, the other slaves followed slowly. There were only ten of them on the Brower place now. The older ones,

like Aunt Kate who worked in the big house, could remember the days when there were more than fifty slaves on the plantation. But that had been a long time ago. And even Jake could remember when there had been a lot more than there were now. A lot of them had been sold, and with the coming of the war some had run away. And those who remained were hoping to get away at the first opportunity.

When they gathered in the yard at the big house, Massa Brower was standing on the porch, his hands gripping the railing tightly. "Well, I guess you must be wondering why I called you out of the fields in the middle of the day." He grinned nervously at the ten expressionless faces below him, faces that were trying to prepare themselves not to feel any emotion when they heard whatever the bad news was. "I don't rightly know how to tell you this. And I guess the only way to say it is just to come out and say it. The South done lost the war. I just heard the news yesterday that General Lee surrendered to the Yankees. So that means that all the slaves is free." He paused a moment, waiting for a reaction, but there was none. ❖

✳ Look over the selection and your Response Notes. Write three sentences or phrases you found that signal change is about to happen. Describe the characters' reactions.

Sentences or phrases that signal change	Characters' reactions
"None of them could remember ever hearing the bell in the afternoon."	They asked each other what it might mean.

✳ Now share your chart with a partner. What words or phrases did your partner notice that you didn't? What new ideas do your partner's words tell you?

....

....

....

....

....

❋ Why do you think there was no reaction from the slaves at the end of the story? What big idea does this tell you?

....

....

....

....

❋ What is one big change that has happened to you or someone you know? How did it affect you or that person?

....

....

....

....

Looking at a character's reaction to change will lead you to big ideas in a text.

When change happens around you, the way you think often changes, too. The same thing happens when you read. You might have certain thoughts at the beginning of a selection. But then you learn about new events, and your thoughts may change by the end. Studying changing events in a story can lead you to **synthesize** new understandings.

This excerpt is from the nonfiction book *The Great Serum Race*. This true story took place in Alaska, during the bitterly cold winter of 1925. As you read, underline text that describes key events in the selection. In the **Response Notes**, write your thoughts about each event.

Response Notes

from The Great Serum Race
by Debbie S. Miller

At Bluff, Balto and Fox waited for Gunnar Kaasen to adjust the leather harnesses and secure the serum package. Then the pair of leaders heard their musher's shout through the raging wind. Balto and Fox led the strong team of thirteen huskies into the swirling snow. Mile after mile, they trotted steadily toward Nome. During the final leg of the run, the wind assaulted them. A violent gust flipped the sled over, and the dogs went flying.

Gunnar struggled to his feet against the might of the wind. After he fought to untangle the dogs, he checked the sled to make sure the serum was securely fastened. Gunnar felt the bottom of the sled in disbelief. The serum package was gone!

In the dark, he crawled around the sled. Since he couldn't see his surroundings, he took off his mitts and felt through the snow with his bare hands. After more than 600 hard-won miles and twenty teams risking their lives, could it be that the serum was lost forever?

Panicked, Gunnar ran his numb hands across windswept bumps of snow. All he could do was hope. Suddenly, he felt something hard. It was the serum! His frostbitten fingers struggled to tie the package onto the sled. Then the wind-battered team ran off.

They struggled on through the night. With less than twenty miles remaining, two of the dogs ran stiffly and appeared to be freezing. Gunnar anchored the sled and put rabbit-skin covers on the dogs to protect their undersides from frostbite.

Through the darkness, Balto and Fox smelled familiar scents. At last the exhausted team reached Nome. They drove into town as most people slept through the blizzard. When Gunnar knocked on the door, Dr. Welch greeted him with a stunned face. How could a musher and team have fought their way through such a storm?

With stiff hands, Gunnar gave the shocked but thankful doctor the life-saving serum.

Twenty brave mushers and more than 160 strong dogs traveled hundreds of miles in the worst conditions. The incredible relay took less than six days. Four dogs perished and several others grew lame because of the lethal weather. Yet their struggle saved many lives in Nome. ❖

✳ List two key events from the selection. What new understandings do you learn from each one?

Event from selection	New understanding from event

✳ What new understandings does the story give you about the role of dogs in the Arctic?

✳ What scene of the journey could you visualize best? Write about it and explain why you could picture it vividly.

....

....

....

....

....

....

....

✳ How does thinking about big ideas and new understandings make your reading meaningful?

....

....

....

....

....

....

....

As story events change, you create new understandings from and about the text.

A poem usually has fewer words than a story or article, but it still tells a story. Since the author doesn't use many words, you often have to rely on your own thoughts and connections to make sense of the poem.

The poem below tells about a historical event in American history. As you read the poem, think about these questions. They will help you **synthesize** your thoughts to create some big ideas about the poem and the event.

- What's happening in the poem?

- How does this poem fit with what I already know about the first moon landing?

- What connections can I make with this poem?

- What big ideas can I create after reading and thinking about the poem?

Now reread the poem with a partner. Together, underline details that suggest the importance of this historical event. In the **Response Notes**, write why you think each detail is important.

Response Notes

First Men on the Moon
by J. Patrick Lewis

July 20, 1969
That afternoon in mid-July,
Two pilgrims watched from distant space
The Moon ballooning in the sky.
They rose to meet it face-to-face.

Their spidery spaceship *Eagle* dropped
Down gently on the lunar sand.
And when the module's engines stopped,
Cold silence fell across the land.

The first man down the ladder, Neil,
Spoke words that we remember now—
"Small step for man . . ." It made us feel
As if we too were there somehow.

Then Neil planted the flag and Buzz
Collected lunar rocks and dust.
They hopped liked kangaroos because
Of gravity. Or wanderlust.

A quarter million miles away,
One small blue planet watched in awe.
And no one who was there that day
Will soon forget the Moon they saw. ❖

✳ Reread the last stanza of the poem. What big ideas
do you think the poet wants you to understand from
this stanza?

....

....

....

....

....

✳ How do you think this event changed people's
thoughts and feelings about space travel? Explain.

....

....

....

....

※ What facts about the moon are woven into the poem? What other facts do you know about the moon?

Facts about the moon in the poem	Other facts about the moon

※ Would you have wanted to be on the first trip to the moon? How would you have felt about the risk? Explain.

....

....

....

....

....

....

Combining thoughts of your own experience with thoughts about historical events will lead you to big ideas.

....

....

The **setting** of a story is where and when it takes place. The setting can also affect the characters in a story. Studying how the characters react to the setting can lead you to **synthesize** big ideas about the text.

This excerpt from the novel *Catwings* is about a family of flying cats. The mother forces her kittens to leave their city home because she thinks it's unsafe. There were too many cars, hungry dogs, and not enough food. The kittens take a long journey to find a new place to live.

As you read, underline details that describe the settings. In the **Response Notes**, write thoughts or questions about the settings.

from Catwings by Ursula K. Le Guin

As Thelma, Roger, James, and Harriet flew on, all they could see beneath them, mile after mile, was the city's roofs, the city's streets.

A pigeon came swooping up to join them. It flew along with them, peering at them uneasily from its little, round, red eye. "What kind of birds are you, anyways?" it finally asked.

"Passenger pigeons," James said promptly.

Harriet mewed with laughter.

The pigeon jumped in mid-air, stared at her, and then turned and swooped away from them in a great, quick curve.

"I wish I could fly like that," said Roger.

"Pigeons are really dumb," James muttered.

"But my wings ache already," Roger said, and Thelma said, "So do mine. Let's land somewhere and rest."

Little Harriet was already heading down towards a church steeple.

They clung to the carvings on the church roof, and got a drink of water from the roof gutters.

"Sitting in the catbird seat!" sang Harriet, perched on a pinnacle.

Response Notes

"It looks different over there," said Thelma, pointing her nose to the west. "It looks softer."

They all gazed earnestly westward, but cats don't see the distance clearly.

"Well, if it's different, let's try it," said James, and they set off again. They could not fly with untiring ease, like the pigeons. Mrs. Tabby had always seen to it that they ate well, and so they were quite plump, and had to beat their wings hard to keep their weight aloft. They learned how to glide, not beating their wings, letting the wind bear them up; but Harriet found gliding difficult, and wobbled badly.

After another hour or so they landed on the roof of a huge factory, even though the air there smelled terrible, and there they slept for a while in a weary, furry heap. Then, towards nightfall, very hungry—for nothing gives an appetite like flying—they woke and flew on.

The sun set. The city lights came on, long strings and chains of lights below them, stretching out towards darkness. Towards darkness they flew, and at last, when around them and under them everything was dark except for one light twinkling over the hill, they descended slowly from the air and landed on the ground.

A soft ground—a strange ground! The only ground they knew was pavement, asphalt, cement. This was all new to them, dirt, earth, dead leaves, grass, twigs, mushrooms, worms. It all smelled extremely interesting. A little creek ran nearby. They heard the song of it and went to drink, for they were very thirsty. After drinking, Roger stayed crouching on the bank, his nose almost in the water, his eyes gazing.

"What's that in the water?" he whispered.

The others came and gazed. They could just make out something moving in the water, in the starlight—a silvery flicker, a gleam. Roger's paw shot out. . . .

"I think it's dinner," he said.

After dinner, they curled up together again under a bush and fell asleep. But first Thelma, then Roger, then James, and then small Harriet, would lift their head, open an eye, listen a moment, on guard. They knew they had come to a much better place than the alley, but they also knew that every place is dangerous, whether you are a fish, or a cat, or even a cat with wings. ❖

✳ Pick two settings from the cats' journey. How does each setting affect the cats?

Setting	How does it affect the cats?

✳ What inferences can you make about the cats' life in the city?

✳ Reread the last sentence of the selection. Why might the cats' new setting be better than the city? Why might it be worse?

Notice how the characters react to the setting. This will lead you to new understandings about the characters and the text.

Aconversation between two people is called a **dialogue**. Dialogues often tell you a lot about characters. By studying dialogues, you can **synthesize** big ideas about the characters and the text.

In the selection below, Gloria and her father solve a problem through their dialogue. Gloria's thinking also changes during the dialogue. As you read, underline text that shows changes in Gloria's thinking. In the **Response Notes**, write how Gloria's thinking has changed.

from **A Rock in the Road** by Ann Cameron

After dinner, my dad washed dishes and I dried. It felt nice to be with him.

"How was school today?" he asked.

I wanted to tell him it wasn't fine, but I couldn't. Because he would think I should understand fractions and I didn't.

"It was fine," I said.

I am not used to talking to my dad. I practically never talk to him, because there is no time.

The reason is Quick Kitchens. Quick Kitchens is my dad's business. All day long, he works in other people's houses, installing new kitchens. When he comes home, he is tired. Then, after dinner, he goes to the answering machine. He plays back all the messages on it about Quick Kitchens, and then he returns the people's calls.

"How much time do you spend in your kitchen?" he asks them. They answer something I can't hear, and then he says, "Once you install a Quick Kitchen, you'll finish your kitchen chores in a fraction of the time."

I didn't used to know what "fraction" meant, but I still hated it. To me it was just a poor word that kept getting hauled out and dragged around and dragged around till it was all worn out.

Response Notes

"Well, I'm glad school was good," my dad said. He rinsed the last dish and I dried it.

"Thanks for helping," he said. "Time to go check the machine."

In a second he would click the answering machine on. In a second all the new Quick Kitchen messages would start pouring out into our old kitchen and he would write down all the numbers to call back. And I would never talk to him.

"Daddy!" I said.

"What, honey?"

I wouldn't have said it like I did, but it just spilled out.

"I hate Quick Kitchens!" I said. "I hate listening to the answering machine. I hate the people's voices, and I hate it when you call them back, and I hate it when you say, 'You will finish your kitchen chores in a fraction of the time.'"

My dad stayed very quiet. I was scared that he was mad.

Then he reached out and took my hand. "I get sick of Quick Kitchens myself, sometimes," he said softly. "Let's you and me sit down and talk."

We sat down at the kitchen table.

"I have to answer the calls," my dad explained. "It's how I get new business. I will try not to say things the same way all the time. I make so many calls, after a while I don't even hear myself."

"It just keeps going on and on," I said.

"Sometimes life is like that," my dad said. "But change always comes."

"Another thing," I said. "I am stupid and I hate fractions. I don't understand them, and I'm the only one in my math class who doesn't get them, and I don't even know why."

I put my head down on the table. My dad lifted it up.

"Gloria," he said. "You're not stupid."

"Then why don't I get it?"

"Everybody has things they don't get," my dad said.

"Everybody?" I repeated. It seemed there must be somebody who got absolutely everything—but for sure it wasn't me.

"It's like this," my dad said. "Everybody's got a different road in life. And for a while you may go along your road just fine, and then all of a sudden there's a rock—a rock so big you can't get by. You can't climb over it, you can't go around it. All you can do is just stand and study it and think and think and think. And then, all of a sudden, you understand it. And then that rock disappears and you can move again."

"Julian doesn't have a rock in his road. Latisha doesn't have a rock in her road," I said.

"You don't know," my dad said. "Everyone does at one time or another. It may not be fractions, but it will be something."

"Fractions is a rock that won't disappear," I said. "Fractions is going to be the next two months, at least."

"Fractions won't disappear," my dad said, "but when you understand them, they won't be a rock in your road. They will be different. Just a pebble or a grain of sand that you'll pass by." ❖

✳ Think about Gloria in the beginning, middle, and end of the selection. What was she like in each part? Write your thoughts in the chart.

What was Gloria like in the beginning?	How do you know?

What was Gloria like in the middle?	How do you know?

What was Gloria like at the end?	How do you know?

✳ What was Gloria surprised to learn about her father's job? How did this affect her feelings about fractions?

....

....

....

....

✳ What kind of journey did Gloria take? How did it help
her deal with her problem?

....

....

....

....

✳ What connections to your own life do you make with
Gloria and her experiences?

....

....

....

....

✳ Explain to a partner what synthesis is. Now write the
three most important points from your conversation.

....

....

....

....

Thinking about
characters' conversations
will help you discover big
ideas about the text.

GLOSSARY

achievement a successful performance

admiring pleased

afford have enough money

apartment complex a group of apartments

barren lifeless

bellow yell loudly

beneficial helpful

bulky big and heavy

buoyant able to float

camellias flowers with a heavy scent

casserole a baked dish

chores household jobs

cicadas insects that make a loud noise

clenched clamped together

colored African American (a term used through the 1960s)

commenced started

confusion lack of order

customs traditions

cutting station where haircuts take place

debt amount owed

declined said "no"

deed a paper showing ownership

delayed late

deluge flood

determination strength of mind

discrimination unfair treatment because of differences

displayed shown

disrupted created confusion

disturb bother

doubtful not certain

dunes sandy hills

earnestly seriously

ecosystem an environment and its life forms

epidemic a widespread outbreak of a disease

essential very important

evidence objects and statements involved in a crime

exposed touched by air or light

fallout small particles of rock or ash

fare amount paid to ride

fast tight

ferocity wildness

fertilize add something to the soil to help plants grow

flashed showed light suddenly

flexible able to bend and move easily

flitting teasing

floundered struggled

food chain a series of life forms in which each eats the next lower member of the series

fraction a small amount

fragile easily harmed

genius very smart

Great Depression a period of time in the 1920s and 1930s when the U.S. economy was doing very badly

gulped swallowed loudly

hauling carrying

hesitated paused

homeland place where a person was born

Iditarod a yearly dog race in Alaska

immigrants people who move from one country to another

install put something in place and ready to use

instantaneous immediate

integrated opened to people of all races

launch start

lemmings small rodents

lunar having to do with the moon

lure to attract

marshals government officers

marshes grassy wetlands

Massa master

matted tangled or knotted

mimicked copied

missionary one who travels to spread religion

module a part of a spacecraft

mushers the people who control sled dogs

mysterious unexplained

N, O

notions ideas

ol' old

orneriness stubbornness or bad-tempered behavior

P

padded protected

passion strong feeling

pellets small balls of matter

periodic declines a decrease in numbers that happens regularly

pinnacle the very top

pollinated when pollen from one plant is used to fertilize another plant

pouting fussing

preacher a church leader who gives sermons

precautions ways to be careful

precious very valuable or prized

predator one that eats other animals

propel move forward

R

reggae a musical form from the Caribbean

rigors difficulties

S

serum fluid that will help prevent a disease

scooped picked up

scrunched crushed or crunched

scuffing dragging one's feet

shifts work hours

shrapnel pieces of an exploding shell

snouts animals' noses

strained nervous

swept moved quickly

T

tennies tennis shoes

trestle a framework that supports a bridge

tripod three-legged holder

U, V, W

unbearable impossible to stand

unconscious not awake because of illness or injury

unforgettable easily remembered

vendors sellers

wake the track left by something moving through water

8 From *The Adventures of Spider: West African Folk Tales* retold by Joyce Cooper Arkhurst. Copyright © 1992. Reprinted by permission of Hachette Book Group USA.

16 "Dreams," copyright © 1994 by The Estate of Langston Hughes, from *The Collected Poems of Langston Hughes* by Langston Hughes, edited by Arnold Rampersad with David Roessel, Associate Editor. Used by permission of Alfred A. Knopf, a division of Random House, Inc.

19, 22 Reprinted with the permission of Simon & Schuster Books for Young Readers, an imprint of Simon & Schuster Children's Publishing Division from *Uncle Jed's Barbershop* by Margaree King Mitchell. Text copyright © 1993 by Margaree King Mitchell.

27 From *Sixteen Years In Sixteen Seconds: The Sammy Lee Story*. Text copyright © 2005. Permission arranged with Lee & Low Books Inc., NY, NY 10016

31 From *Julian, Dream Doctor* by Ann Cameron. Copyright © 1990. Reprinted with permission by Random House Inc.

35 "The Knee-High Man", from *The Knee-High Man and Other Tales* by Julius Lester, copyright © 1972 by Julius Lester. Used by permission of Dial Books for Young Readers, A Division of Penguin Young Readers Group, A Member of Penguin Group (USA) Inc., 345 Hudson Street, New York, NY 10014. All rights reserved.

40 Reprinted with the permission of Simon & Schuster Books for Young Readers, an imprint of Simon & Schuster Children's Publishing Division from *Frindle* by Andrew Clements. Text copyright © 1996 Andrew Clements.

44 "The Many and the Few" Copyright © 1999 by J. Patrick Lewis. First appeared in *Lives: Poems about Famous Americans*, published by HarperCollins. Reprinted by permission of Curtis Brown, Ltd.

47 From *Through My Eyes* by Ruby Bridges. Copyright © 1998 by Ruby Bridges.

52, 57 From *A Dog Called Kitty* by Bill Wallace. Copyright © 1980 by Bill Wallace. All rights reserved. Reprinted by permission of Holiday House, Inc.

61 Excerpt from "Frontier Schools", from *Children Of The Wild West* by Russell Freedman. Copyright © 1983 by Russell Freedman. Reprinted by permission of Clarion Books, an imprint of Houghton Mifflin Company. All rights reserved.

66 From "Apple Blossoms" by Terry Trueman. Reprinted by permission of SLL/Sterling Lord Literistic, Inc. Copyright by Terry Trueman.

72 "Snowy Owl" from *Birds Of Prey* by Jonathan P. Latimer and Karen Stray Nolting, illustrated by Roger Tory Peterson. Copyright © 1999 by Houghton Mifflin Company. Reprinted by permission of Kingfisher Publications Plc., an imprint of Houghton Mifflin Company. All rights reserved.

76 Excerpt from *Forensics* by Richard Platt. Copyright © Kingfisher Publications Plc 2005. Reprinted by permission of Kingfisher Publications Plc., an imprint of Houghton Mifflin Company. All rights reserved.

80 From *Caring For Cheetahs: My African Adventure* by Rosanna Hansen. Reprinted with the permission of Boyds Mills Press, Inc. Text copyright © 2007 by Rosanna Hansen.

84 "Three Cheers for Bats!" Text copyright © 1993 by Laurence Pringle.

89 Text copyright © 2006 by Leslie Bulion, Illustrations copyright © 2006 by Leslie Evans. Used with permission by Charlesbridge Publishing, Inc. All rights reserved.

ILLUSTRATIONS

3–7: Elizabeth Brandt; **8–13:** Justin Parpan; **15:** Elizabeth Brandt; **19 *tr:*** Soud; **20:** Soud; **21:** Aartpack; **25:** Aartpack; **26 *c:*** Aartpack; **26 *b:*** Soud; **26:** Soud; **28:** Dan Santat; **30:** Aartpack **35:** Annie Lunsford; **36, 37:** Annie Lunsford; **39:** Elizabeth Brandt; **40, 41:** Dan Santat; **43:** Dan Santat; **46:** Aartpack; **51:** Aartpack; **53:** Dan Grant; **57, 58:** Dan Grant; **65:** Elizabeth Brandt; **67, 68:** Helen Dardik; **73:** Aartpack; **81 *c:*** Jean Wisenbaugh; **81 *l:*** Jean Wisenbaugh; **81 *r:*** Aartpack; **90 *tr:*** © Dorling Kindersley/Getty Images; **90 *tl:*** © Dorling Kindersley/Getty Images; **90 *bl:*** © Dorling Kindersley/Getty Images; **90 *br:*** © Dorling Kindersley/Getty Images; **90 *c:*** Aartpack; **93:** Elizabeth Brandt; **95:** Dan Santat; **105:** Carrie English; **119:** Elizabeth Brandt; **123 *l:*** Aartpack **123 *r:*** Aartpack **130:** Aartpack **131:** Robert McGuire; **137:** © Vadym Nechyporenko/Fotolia; **138:** Anna Wadham; **141:** Anna Wadham; **143:** Elizabeth Brandt; **144, 145:** Carrie English; **146:** Carrie English; **159, 160:** Anna Wadham.

PHOTOGRAPHY

Photo Research by AARTPACK, Inc.

Cover, 0: © Ken Usami/Photodisc/Getty Images; **1:** © Ken Usami/Photodisc/Getty Images.

Unit 1 16 *t:* © Photowood Inc./Photowood Inc./Corbis; **16 *b:*** © Bloomimage/Corbis; **17:** © Floresco Productions/Corbis; **18:** © Bloomimage/Corbis; **19 *bl:*** © Jim Allan/Alamy; **21 *t:*** © CORBIS **22:** © Dana Bartekoske/Fotolia; **23:** © Duncan Smith/Photodisc/Getty Images; **24 *c:*** © Andy Sotiriou/Photodisc/Getty Images; **24 *bl:*** © ValGo/Fotolia; **25:** © Getty Images;

26: © Photowood Inc./Photowood Inc./Corbis; **27:** © FPG/Hulton Archive/Getty Images; **29:** © Jacques Palut/Fotolia; **29 *t:*** © bluestockin/istockphoto; **30:** © zouzou48/Fotolia; **31 *tr:*** © Image Source/Corbis; **31 *b:*** © George Doyle/Stockbyte/Getty Images; **32:** © Goodshoot/Corbis; **34:** © Hallgerd/Fotolia; **35 *b:*** © Elena Aliaga/Fotolia; **38:** © Bloomimage/Corbis.

Unit 2 42: © Comstock Images/Alamy; **44, 45:** © Time & Life Pictures/Getty Images; **46:** © javarman/Fotolia; **47, 48:** © Bettmann/CORBIS; **49 *b:*** © Bettmann/CORBIS; **49 *c:*** © Pedro Tavares/Fotolia; **50 *b:*** © devon/Fotolia; **50 *t:*** © Igor Negovelov/Fotolia; **52:** © iofoto/Fotolia; **55 *t:*** © Brand X Pictures/Alamy; **55 *b:*** © Marek Zuk/Alamy; **56:** © Scott Waby/Fotolia; **59:** © Orlando Marra/Workbook Stock/Jupiter Images; **60 *t:*** © James Steidl/Fotolia; **60 *b:*** © Sergey Shlyaev/Fotolia; **61:** © Tom Morrison/The Image Bank/Getty Images; **62:** © CORBIS; **63 *tl:*** © Shirley Hu Xiao Fang/Fotolia; **63 *bl:*** © Mona Makela/Fotolia; **63 *br:*** © Richard Cano/Fotolia; **63 *tr:*** © Ablestock/Inmagine; **63 *bc:*** © Purestock/Getty Images; **64:** © Victor Potasyev/Fotolia; **54, 55:** © tracy tucker/istockphoto.

Unit 3 66: © Royalty Free/Corbis/Jupiter Images; **70:** © philippe Devanne/Fotolia; **71 *b:*** © Image Source Pink/Image Source/Getty Images **71 *t:*** © philippe Devanne/Fotolia; **72 *t:*** © Jim Wehtje/Brand X Pictures/Jupiter Images; **72 *b:*** © Marina Krasnovid/Fotolia; **73 *l:*** © Graham Wren/Oxford Scientific/Jupiter Images; **73 *r:*** © Kennan Ward/CORBIS; **74:** © Jim Wehtje/Brand X Pictures/Jupiter Images; **75 *b:*** © Ingram Publishing/Jupiter Images; **75 *t:*** © Daniel Cox/Oxford Scientific/Jupiter Images **76:** © Leah-anne Thompson/Fotolia; **77:** © Njari/

INDEX